The Conservation of Georgian Edinburgh

The Conservation of Georgian Edinburgh

The Proceedings and Outcome of a Conference organized by The Scottish Civic Trust in Association with The Edinburgh Architectural Association and in conjunction with The Civic Trust, London edited by Sir Robert Matthew, John Reid, and Maurice Lindsay at the University of Edinburgh Press

© 1972
EDINBURGH UNIVERSITY PRESS
22 George Square, Edinburgh
ISBN 0 85224 215 8
North America
Aldine · Atherton, Inc.
529 South Wabash Avenue, Chicago
Library of Congress Catalog
Card Number 72-77764
Printed in Great Britain by
The Kynoch Press, Birmingham

Contents

List of Illustrations

Preface

The Rt Hon. Viscount Muirshiel, CH, CMG

This book is the record of a remarkable exercise in voluntary effort in an admirable cause. It tells the story of crucial moves towards conserving one of the largest, most distinguished examples of town design in Europe; a story which must result in partnership between owners, residents, Local and Central Government, if it is to reach its proper conclusion.

The story begins in May, 1967, when the Scottish Civic Trust came into existence at a ceremony in the University of Glasgow. The prime aim of the Scottish Civic Trust is to stimulate, throughout Scotland, interest in and concern for environment. This voluntary body with charitable status is financed by industry, commerce, family Trusts, and individual bequests and donations. A list of its Trustees is printed elsewhere in this book.

At the conclusion of the inaugural ceremony one of the Trustees, the architect Sir Robert Matthew, remarked to the Director of the Trust, Mr Maurice Lindsay, and myself that we must 'do something about the New Town of Edinburgh'. Without either of us fully realizing the 'something' Sir Robert had in mind, we both agreed.

Over the next few weeks, it became apparent that before any constructive steps could be taken to ensure the conservation of the two hundred year old 'New Town' of Edinburgh, a survey of the fabric of all the buildings in the area must be made. Few even of the residents in the 'New Town' realized the extent of the damage which time and the elements had caused to the stone work, balconies, and other details.

Estimates of the extent of the damage and of the probable cost of repairing that damage were essential if financial aid was to be sought from Central and Local Government to carry out a task of conservation which from the outset, it was clear, must be beyond the resources of many of the owners and residents. The justification for seeking such financial help was, of course, the recognition that Georgian Edinburgh is far more than a personal or local possession. It forms an integral part of our whole European architectural heritage. The decision to confine the survey to the fabric of the buildings was deliberate—Edinburgh Corporation, with a full sense of its responsibilities, had already commissioned a detailed study of the New Town's traffic problems, so closely related to successful conservation, and was fully aware of the related planning implications.

From the start it had been accepted that a major Conference must be mounted in Edinburgh to establish in Edinburgh, in Scotland, and for that matter throughout the United Kingdom and Europe, a proper appreciation of the significance of the New Town, the problems with which it was faced, and the practical steps which could and must be taken for its conservation.

Accordingly a Conference Committee was formed under the chairmanship of Sir Robert Matthew and 6 June 1970 was fixed as the date for the Conference. An approach to the Edinburgh Architectural Association produced an immediate response in the shape of an undertaking, not only to carry out a survey of the external fabric of some five thousand properties, but also to make a photographic record of each building, all on a voluntary basis. More than one hundred and forty architects, surveyors, photographers, and others freely gave of their time and skills, and over a period of almost two years, their task was completed. Their names are listed in the Appendix.

When the results of the Survey became available, an Assessment Group was formed to consider the financial implications of the findings, and what involvement of Local and Central Government might reasonably be recommended. In the event, the advice of this Group, whose names are also listed in Appendix 2 was largely accepted by the Conference, by Edinburgh Corporation, and by the Scottish Office.

The Conference, with the title *The Conservation of Georgian Edinburgh*, took place as planned, and on 6 June 1970, in the Assembly Rooms, George Street, Edinburgh—themselves a splendid example of civic architecture in Georgian Edinburgh—some eleven hundred people arrived at ten in the morning and stayed until five-thirty in the evening, listening to speeches and taking part in a general discussion. This book is a record of the Conference and of its conclusions. A second part will present the essential survey material. Together, both parts should provide valuable material for students of architecture and planning concerned with conservation throughout the civilized world.

This book implicitly and explicitly is a warrant for the effort and money that must be expended so that this architectural heritage can survive and continue as an essential and living entity within the total fabric of the City. The statements, debates, and the resolutions passed by the Conference, bear witness to the concern of those who took part for securing the Georgian town against the effects of age and weather, and also of modern developments. It is hoped that a second volume will set out through text and illustration a record of what is required for the repair and restoration of streets and buildings. The ultimate guarantors, however, of the whole project, are the occupants of the buildings;

Edinburgh people, whose will it clearly is that the buildings of the New Town and other buildings of the period, those visual reminders of civilized values, must survive.

Nothing could underline the international as well as national importance of the Conference more strongly than the welcome given to the delegates by the Lord Provost of Edinburgh and the presence of Count Sforza, Deputy Secretary General of the Council of Europe; of Monsieur Sorlin, the Inspector General for Sites and Historic Monuments at the Ministry of Cultural Affairs in Paris; of Lord Hughes, Minister of State in the Scottish Office who deputized for the Secretary of State; Lord Holford, Professor Colin Buchanan, Sir John Betjeman, Professor Patrick Nuttgens, Professor A. J. Youngson, and Andrew Kerr. Sir Robert Matthew, who presented the report to the Conference, has since been appointed Adviser on Conservation to the Secretary of State for Scotland. The importance of the Conservation of Georgian Edinburgh to the nation was further acknowledged by messages from His Royal Highness, Prince Philip, Duke of Edinburgh, from Her Majesty Queen Elizabeth the Queen Mother, and from Duncan Sandys, President both of the Civic Trust and of Europa Nostra.

That Georgian Edinburgh was of European consequence was made fully evident in the speeches of Count Sforza and Monsieur Sorlin. The ready grasp by the audience that this was their heritage which was being honoured was deeply gratifying to the organizers of the Conference and, perhaps above all, to those whose work had culminated in the meetings. The Survey on which the Conference was based was the major contribution of The Edinburgh Architectural Association. The team was led by Mr John Reid. Behind them as it were, was the Chairman of the Conference Committee, Sir Robert Matthew, whose concept the Conference was and whose urge produced it. He in turn was supported by the Scottish Civic Trust, under its Director, Mr Maurice Lindsay, with substantial help from the London Office of the Civic Trust.

In his opening address to the Conference, the Lord Provost of Edinburgh properly drew attention to the restoration and preservation of the Royal Mile and other similar achievements in Edinburgh which Edinburgh Town Council had authorized. The Lord Provost expressed his gratitude to the voluntary bodies in the City for their help. Thus, at the outset, the Conference was apprised of the warmth with which the Civic Authority welcomes participation in the task of conserving the historic city. Opening with authoritative and professional expositions of the case leading to questions and statements from the floor, the Conference itself was an example of democratic procedures. At the end, the opinion of the meeting was expressed in this Resolution:

That this Conference welcomes the Report on the Conservation of Georgian Edinburgh, submitted by the Conference Committee under the Chairmanship of Sir Robert Matthew, warmly congratulates the authors, re-emphasizes the unique importance of Georgian Edinburgh to our national and international architectural heritage, and calls upon the Scottish Civic Trust to start forthwith negotiations for the setting up of an advisory committee as recommended in the Report so that the necessary steps may be taken, with the practical and financial support of Central Government and the Local Authority, to achieve the conservation of Georgian Edinburgh along the lines indicated in the Report, and in the light of the views expressed during this Conference.

The Conference further calls upon all bodies concerned in the meantime and until such new arrangements can be made to use to the maximum the powers and grants already available for the conservation of the New Town.

During the summer months of 1970, the Scottish Civic Trust discharged the responsibility placed upon it by the foregoing Resolution, conducting negotiations for the setting up of the recommended body with Edinburgh Amenity Societies, with Edinburgh Corporation, and with the Scottish Development Department of the Government. The outcome was that on 22 December 1970, at a meeting in the Scottish Office conducted by the Parliamentary Under-Secretary for Development, the Hon. George Younger, it was agreed that the Edinburgh New Town Conservation Committee, with the following representation, should be set up under the Chairmanship of the former Lord Provost of Edinburgh, Sir John Greig Dunbar:

Edinburgh Corporation	6 representatives
Historic Buildings Council For Scotland . .	4 representatives
Scottish Development Dept.	1 representative
Sir Robert Matthew (as Secretary of State's Adviser on Conservation Policy). . .	1 representative
The Scottish Civic Trust	1 representative
The Scottish Georgian Society . . .	1 representative
The Cockburn Association (The Edinburgh Civic Trust)	1 representative
The New Town Residents Associations . .	3 representatives

At the time of writing, the Committee has been set up, and for the first year, the Government has intimated a grant of £50,000, and Edinburgh Corporation a grant of £25,000. The proportion to be carried by owners must obviously vary according to circumstances, but the broad principle of Central and Local Government contributions on a two-to-one basis has been accepted. All concerned are well aware that these initial amounts will inevitably increase from the second year onwards.

The Scottish Civic Trust has recommended that the Committee should appoint its own Director, and that it should seek to raise a substantial private fund from national and international sources, so that it may be in a position to give interest-free loans where necessary, or purchase, restore, and re-sell individual houses on a revolving fund; methods of operation which, under existing legislation are not possible with Central or Local Government funds.

The whole operation has been a remarkable example of public involvement in a project, the outcome of which is likely to bring satisfaction and delight to forthcoming generations of Edinburgh citizens and to people from many lands.

As Chairman of the Scottish Civic Trust, and of the Conference on 6 June 1970, I should like to pay special tribute to Sir Robert Matthew, whose vision, foresight, and determination resulted in the undertaking of the operation; to the Edinburgh Architectural Association's survey team led by Mr John Reid, without whose work the Conference could not have been held; to the Historic Buildings Council represented at the Conference by Lord Stratheden, its Chairman, who spoke of the excitement he shared in the concept of the new conservation areas; and the National Trust for Scotland, who provided interim financial assistance; to those who provided the financial subsidy necessary for the publication of this book, namely the Pilgrim Trust, the Marc Fitch Fund, the Carnegie Trust, Sir James Miller, Messrs John M. Geoghegan & Co., Chartered Accountants, Messrs Baillie, Gifford & Co., L. M. Harper Gow, Esq., Mr E. J. Ivory of Ivory & Sim, The Directors of James Allan & Son Ltd, Scottish & Newcastle Breweries Ltd, W. S. McIntosh-Reid, Esq., Messrs James Gray & Son, Messrs W. & J. Burness, ws, Messrs Melroses Limited, Messrs Pillans & Wilson, The Scottish American Investment Company Limited, John Bartholomew & Son Ltd, Messrs Jenners, Edinburgh University Press and its Secretary, Mr A. R. Turnbull, for their willingness to undertake this important but complicated publication, and to Dr Helen Muirhead, their editor, who bore the brunt of the day-to-day editorial work: to Mr George Bruce and Mr George Scott-Moncrieff who gave literary assistance to Sir Robert Matthew, Mr John Reid, and Mr Maurice Lindsay, the Editorial Committee; and to all those who contributed in any way to the success of the operation.

Whatever else it may undertake in the future, it is unlikely that the Scottish Civic Trust will ever again find itself involved in an exercise of such magnitude. It is a matter of pride and satisfaction to me, as its first Chairman, that it should have been involved in an operation which has so positively asserted Scotland's belief in civilized values.

The publishers gratefully acknowledge the following sources of illustrations in the book: Bath Corporation; Mr John Dewar; Edinburgh Corporation (City Architect and Town Planning Departments); Sir Robert Matthew; Mr John Reid; the late Mr Edwin Smith; M. François Sorlin, Miss Diane Tammas; The Venice in Peril Fund; and Messrs E. R. Yerbury and Son.

1. Melville Street, looking west

When the Scottish Civic Trust was founded in May 1967 one of its trustees, Sir Robert Matthew, urged that it should make the fabric of the *New Town* of Edinburgh one of its most urgent concerns.

The *New Town*, dating fron 1767, remains a unique example of Georgian town planning and distinguished architecture, and over the years it has grown in international fame. Yet, though it has remained remarkably intact, its external condition is now deteriorating rapidly, and is subject to heavy pressures of various kinds. Even before the passing of the Civic Amenities Act (1967)—and through it the creation of the Conservation Area concept—it had become clear that a cooperation of interests similar to that which originally produced the New Town would be needed if its fabric were to be conserved and its vitality maintained, while continuing to serve the modern needs of those who use it.

The moment seemed ripe. The Melville Street/Melville Crescent pilot   *1* project instituted by the Historic Buildings Council for Scotland and Edinburgh Corporation had been launched as the first preservation project in the joint operation by the HBC and Corporation. During the 1968 Edinburgh International Festival the exhibition '200 Summers in a City' had greatly aroused public interest in the history and architectural merit of the New Town.

2. The City Chambers, originally the Royal Exchange

Accordingly, the Trustees, as soon as possible, sought the collaboration of the Edinburgh Architectural Association which, first under the Presidency of Mr James Dunbar-Nasmith and then under that of Mr B.V.K. Cottier, mustered a team of over one hundred and twenty architects, surveyors, engineers, and others, who volunteered to give of their time and skills to carry out an external fabric survey of every property in a pre-designated area of over two hundred streets, comprising the concentrated centre of Edinburgh's Georgian development.

It was decided to present a summary of the findings to a Conference, convened in Edinburgh, to be attended by representatives of national and local government, by conservation and amenity societies, and by owners and occupiers of New Town property.

The conference was held in the Assembly Rooms, Edinburgh, on 6 June 1970, with the Right Honourable Viscount Muirshiel in the Chair. The present volume derives from that conference, and presents an edited and illustrated version of the Proceedings.

The following message from *His Royal Highness The Prince Philip, Duke of Edinburgh* was communicated to the conference:

Anyone who has seen the work of the Civic Trust anywhere in the British Isles must realize what an important contribution it is making to

3. The City Chambers in 1885, with the arcaded front filled in with shops

4. The City Chambers today, after restoration

the visual improvement of our towns and cities. That the Scottish Civic Trust has decided to tackle the New Town of Edinburgh is splendid news. It is always sad when some well-loved and familiar building disappears to make way for improvements but it would be a disaster if this unique piece of large-scale town planning and architecture were to be allowed

2-4 to decay. The problem of conserving these buildings and of giving them a new lease of life is not going to be easy, but the effort is well worth making, and I hope it will, indeed it must succeed.'

The Private Secretary to *Her Majesty the Queen Mother* communicated to Viscount Muirshiel, and through him to the conference, that
'The Queen Mother . . . has asked me to tell you how deeply she feels on the whole question of the conservation of the New Town of Edinburgh. It is very much a matter close to Her Majesty's heart.'

In opening the conference, the *Lord Provost of Edinburgh*, the Rt Hon. J. W. McKay, spoke as follows:

'To me, "conservation" is a relatively new word but "preservation" is, I think, much better known—at least within the City Chambers—

5, 6 because we have seen the restoration and preservation of the *Royal Mile*.
7 We have seen the rehabilitation of the village of *Swanston*. We have seen
8 *Cramond Village*, too, looking a lot better for the attentions of the local authority. The guidelines for these works were laid down by a former City architect and we remember gratefully the work he did for the City at a time when only the plans could be drawn but the work could not be fulfilled, so he has not had the opportunity of seeing the results of his farsightedness. At the same time there was echoed in Mr McRae's work some of the ideas and thoughts which he contributed to the Abercrombie Plan (1949) and again, of course, in the current development. But now with the *Civic Amenities Act* (1967) we come to a new concept in planning, a more overall and positive approach to the problem. At present, there are eight areas under review and it is appropriate that the first— Zone One—is the *New Town*. I would like to say, on behalf of Edinburgh Corporation, how grateful we are for all the voluntary help and assistance we have received from the various interested organizations. The voluntary survey has been a colossal task and many people have spent, I am sure, many long hours on behalf of the community. I hope that this work will not go unrecognized in the future. *Designation*, of course, itself is the key, and while it would not initially cost the Corporation anything, there *are* financial considerations, not only in regard to the global sum but also perhaps in the sharing of the expenditure. We must have a realistic estimate of the cost and thereafter we must have realistic talks, perhaps a series of talks, about the sharing of the burden. I trust these

5. Chessel's Court, before restoration

6. Chessel's Court restored

7. Part of Swanston Village restored

8. Cottages at Cramond from across the River Almond

talks and this decision will not be long delayed because, speaking for myself as owner of a property — a business property — in the New Town, I have the highest regard for this kind of living, these kinds of buildings, and I think it would be a mistake if we allowed things to drift. This, to my mind, is the time for going ahead and taking action. It's going to be a partnership, as I see it, between the Government, the local authority, and the owners, and we cannot regard the owners or even the local authority as more than trustees for this great heritage. This, to my mind, is essentially and basically a national problem, because this is a national heritage.'

Lord Hughes, Under-Secretary of State at the Scottish Office, in addressing the conference, and speaking on behalf of the Government, said:

'It is tremendously encouraging to see such a large gathering here today to discuss the problems of Georgian Edinburgh. Particularly is this so with so many distinguished speakers coming to pay their respects to this great City and to participate in discussions about its future. It is a remarkable demonstration of the depth of feeling that there is in all quarters about the quality of Georgian Edinburgh and the vital need to ensure its conservation. This depth of feeling is something which presents the Government and Edinburgh Corporation with an inspiring challenge. I am confident that no Government will flinch from the responsibility of playing its part in safeguarding this great asset. It is an asset which is priceless, not only in aesthetic but also in economic terms. The New Town is an essential part of the unique character of the city.

Population increases, more and more cars come on to our roads, living standards rise, the demands of commerce and industry grow in every direction. As a result, both local and central government face extreme difficulty in adapting, to the needs of a modern society, the towns and cities which were built for the very different needs of a bygone age. There has to be this adaptation, this reconciliation of the old and the new. It is important for everyone to accept that the New Town of Edinburgh has to be able to live to survive. We are talking not about preserving a corpse, but looking after and where necessary rejuvenating what is at present essentially a healthy organism. Indeed, it is a remarkable tribute to those who designed its gracious buildings and planned its spacious layout and also to the quality of the stone with which the masons worked, that today the New Town is largely intact and has withstood so well the twentieth-century pressures of traffic, people, and commerce. To ensure its continuation for another two hundred years we need a combination of imaginative planning, and a carefully thought-out scheme of conservation. The decisions to be taken within the next year or two will determine whether or not the New Town will be able to survive both the threats to its integrity and the insidious effects of old age on its fabric. At this stage I would like to make it clear that the principle of a tripartite cost-sharing arrangement with Edinburgh Corporation and owners of properties in the New Town involving a Government contribution is definitely accepted. We have announced our acceptance of a report, one of the recommendations in which is that legislation should be introduced to enable the payment of an entirely new Exchequer grant for historic areas which are made the subject of a new type of general conservation scheme prepared by local authorities. This legislation will obviously be directly relevant to the provision of money for the New Town. It really would be impossible at this stage of consideration to quantify the amount of Government assistance which can be made available but I am sure that any Government would hope to be able to make enough resources available to ensure the success of the scheme. Such assistance would, of course, be an addition to the normal budget of the Historic Buildings Council for Scotland which the Secretary of State has increased by about twenty per cent for this current programme, bringing it up to a total of one-third of a million pounds over the next three years; so we are not, as Governments so very often do, helping a new cause at the expense of taking away from somebody else. What we will do here will, quite definitely, require additional money. I was particularly pleased to see the suggestions in the Conference Report that a joint committee should be formed to oversee the measures taken for conservation in the New Town. This Conference brings home to us, through its sponsorship by the Scottish Civic Trust, by the attendance of representatives of civic societies, street associations and the like, the enormously important part which such bodies can play in helping Central and Local Government to conserve and improve the environment. I hope the practice of bringing responsible civic amenity bodies fully into local authority planning for conservation areas will become widespread. Consultation with such bodies will be a requirement in relation to listed buildings when Part v of the 1967 Act comes into operation. Both the local authorities and the civic bodies concerned must benefit from constructive cooperation and from a greater mutual understanding about each others' problems and points of view.

The next stage of consultation on the details of arrangements designed to secure the conservation of the New Town is a large task and there may be no one simple answer which can be applicable throughout the different areas of the New Town but the ultimate prize is well worth winning and we are ready to help to win it.'

9. Royal Crescent, Bath

10. The north side, Charlotte Square, Edinburgh

A message was read from Mr Duncan Sandys, President of the Civic Trust, and President of *Europa Nostra*. It said:

9, 10 '*Georgian Edinburgh*, by reason of its homogeneous character and extensive area, forms, with Bath, one of the two most outstanding examples of the town planning of its period. It is not only a precious architectural possession of Scotland and of Britain, it is one of the treasures of Europe's cultural heritage. Its preservation and restoration is, of course, largely a financial problem. It is important that full value should be obtained for the money expended and to tackle the task piecemeal would produce unsatisfactory results and in the end cost very much more. For that reason, I am sure that you are being wise to undertake a complete survey of the whole area and to budget and programme the work as a comprehensive exercise. I shall look forward to hearing the outcome of your discussions which will, without doubt, play a powerful part in focussing attention upon this problem and in stimulating action.'

Edinburgh as European Cultural Heritage

It is a very great honour for me to have been asked to come here today to this very important Conference and to address you. I am very impressed by the size of the audience. Having attended other meetings of this kind for other cities as important to the culture and civilization of Europe as Edinburgh—Venice for instance—I must say that none of these meetings *11* has gathered so large an audience. It is a great tribute to this city that so many citizens should recognize the importance of the problem under discussion today, and this is most encouraging—at least as great an encouragement as the words which we have just heard coming from the representative of central government.

You might wonder why a member of the Council of Europe was asked to come and take part in today's meeting. As a European intergovernmental organization concerned with European problems, the Council of Europe has inevitably come round to seeking a policy and solutions to the kind of problem, existing throughout Europe, similar to that confronting Edinburgh today in its 'New Town' section. Unfortunately, just as national policies are always late in meeting the big issues confronting them, just as generals apply to a war the tactics of the previous war, so European policies on the question of conservation have only begun to emerge when the problem has reached a state of crisis. Yet, something at least has been done and it is this *something* which I am called upon to tell you about.

The magnitude of this problem of preservation and rehabilitation of sites and monuments in post-war Europe is such that we should already be much further ahead in solving them than we actually are. By this time there should exist a list, a European list, of those sites and monuments (monuments taken in the broadest sense, the 'New Town' of Edinburgh in this vocabulary being a monument in itself) which deserve, from a European point of view, full preservation, full rehabilitation through European means and with European money—by this time there should already exist a pool of conservationist technicians, and of architects. Policies should already have been devised and a European fund should already be in existence, because the scale of the problems facing such towns in Europe is so great, the pressure—the demographic pressure, the technological pressure—is such that national means, not only national but probably European means, will be necessary. That, of course, is still far ahead of us and we are far from having achieved such ends.

11. Venice in decay

12. Staircase of hôtel de Braque, Paris

What has already been done? First of all, how has the Council of Europe become engaged in these problems? The parliamentary assembly of the Council of Europe, to which Lord Muirshiel has belonged for many years [he has been one of the pre-eminent members of the Consultative Assembly of the Council of Europe to which other Scotsmen, Lord John Hope, William Ross, Maxwell Fyfe (later Lord Kilmuir), and many others have belonged] was the place in which these enormous problems, posed by cities like Venice, like Edinburgh, Bath, Avignon, and more, — though few are on the scale and of the importance of Edinburgh or Venice — were raised. The Consultative Assembly thought that the attention of Governments should be called to the urgency of the problems posed by these cities, and by the rapidly worsening and dramatic circumstances in which these great shrines of culture and of European civilization found themselves. The Council of Europe has therefore acted to attract the attention of national governments to the importance and to the urgency of these problems: of alerting the public opinion of Europe, of promoting new forms of teaching in schools, drawing the attention of children to the importance of their architectural inheritance, in their culture and education. In a more practical and immediate realm, the Council of Europe has incited private organizations — private national organizations — such as the *Civic Trust*, the *National Trust* in the United Kingdom, *Italia Nostra* in Italy, *Les Vieilles Maisons Françaises* in France, the   *12* *Heimatbund* in Switzerland, and other such organizations — to federate and create a European federation of private national movements. This federation has come into being — it is called *Europa Nostra* — and its present Chairman is the Hon. Duncan Sandys, who is a very eminent member of the Consultative Assembly of the Council of Europe and whom I regret is not with us today.

The other practical step was taken by governments — by intergovernmental action, following the pressure of the parliamentary assembly to create a high-powered group of experts of European repute. One of them is here today, M. François Sorlin. The seventeen governments of the Council of Europe have asked this group of experts to devise a policy and to make suggestions for solutions.

Let me tell you in a few words what has been the philosophy of the Council of Europe in this respect and what types of solution are being aimed at. During the last quarter-century great changes have taken place in the attitude of peoples and governments towards their architectural heritage. The days are past when a monument was regarded as a rather dilapidated building worth preserving for sentimental reasons only. Such a romantic outlook led governments to spend money in a very restricted way and only buildings considered to be most valuable or most typical

13. Church of the Madonna dell'Orto, Venice

were adequately maintained at governmental expense. The economic and social changes which have taken place in Europe as the result of the last two wars have had a radical effect on our attitude. On the one hand it has become apparent that many old houses could no longer be used for their original purpose, since their owners had ceased to be in a position to maintain them properly. Another much more serious threat occurred with the uncontrolled growth of towns and industry. Tremendous demands were made on land, often regardless of the need to maintain our cultural heritage. I only mention these now very commonplace ideas because they are the causes of the dramatic situation in which we find ourselves and which has developed so rapidly as to become a real menace, with unforseen consequences for the survival of our civilization.

I would now like to say in a few words what are the basic elements of this European policy devised by the group of experts appointed by the European governments. My first remark is that the policy advocated by the Council of Europe concerns the cultural architectural heritage as a whole: that is, not just the great monuments that are of interest to all Europe or even to the world, but everything that has been bequeathed to us by the past,, including such more modest survivals as country villages, old town quarters, and even whole townships (possessing no historic or artistic monuments but being themselves living witness to the life of past generations). I would like strongly to stress the importance of this approach, since it represents a change in kind, with regard to the situation. I say this with great pleasure since this country has for many years been a forerunner in this respect.

What are the main reasons which have led us to adopt this new approach? I can give you four. There is, first, a *cultural* reason; monuments and sites are part of our cultural heritage. Once demolished and replaced by ephemeral constructions, buildings which are essential relics of the past are irretrievably lost. Should this testimony disappear, *13* archaeologists and historians would lose one of the most important sources of their knowledge of the past. Then there is a *human* reason: the impersonal character of the standardized new buildings makes people aware of their fundamental need to identify with their environment. This identification is possible only if there exists a fundamental harmony between the man-made and the natural environment. This is what characterizes most of our cultural heritage, and explains why there is an increasing private demand for old houses to be restored and used to live in. Probably the most characteristic feature of this trend is that, more and more, it is the younger generation that is seeking this kind of private habitation. Our cultural heritage provides a setting tailored to the measurements of man. This is so true that the town planners of today are

C

14, 15 exploring the towns of the past to discover the secret of a setting on a human scale; for instance, the 'New Town' of Edinburgh, which was once the last word in the achievement of town planners.

What must we do to deal with this situation? During the past twenty-five years—during the whole post-war period—governments, in carrying out their planning policies, have had to take energetic measures to organize on rational lines the economic and social development of their countries. There has been some inevitable neglect of groups and areas of buildings of historic or artistic interest, in the need to deal with the new situation created by the population explosion and the progress of technology. The problem is obviously a complex one, and trial and experiment will be necessary before a solution is found. It is precisely this attempt to suit varying needs, to 'fit in', that is lacking in most of the groups of modern buildings put up under the pressure—the stringent pressure—of demographic and economic demands. Merely by stating this we put our finger on the root of the problem. For the real question is: with whom does, or should, the decision lie? In most cases, until now, decisions have been taken at local level, where the fight between preservationists and advocates of modern amenities has resulted more often than not in victory for the latter. Who can say that a house or a church or a group of buildings has more, or less, importance than a road, than a new housing estate, or a factory which will bring employment to many people? Such questions developed into a sort of blind confrontation between those who wanted progress and those who seemed unduly attracted to the past. Now, my contention is that this is a false dilemma. The question of the best use of the land should be tackled on a much higher level, where the problems are clearly seen, and where experts can weigh up the pros and cons. It might well be that one area should be sacrificed for the sake of a better one elsewhere; but in all cases the architectural heritage must be considered not as a mere survival from the past, but as something valuable, closely connected with our present and, still more, with our future needs.

This brings me to my third point—the *social* factor—which is becoming increasingly important today. One of the most acute needs of our time is the need for housing. When accommodation is in such desperately short supply, it seems wrong to pull down old buildings which could be converted into new houses. It is not for me to tell you here in Scotland, where so much has been done so well, that old houses restored and equipped with modern amenities can become the most sought-after dwellings of today. But this, alas, still remains the exception throughout Europe. The Council of Europe feels that this policy should be applied to whole districts of big cities or even to entire towns. These

14. London, view of St Paul's, by Guardi

15. St Paul's from Waterloo Bridge

16, 17 may have no unique monuments to boast of, yet the proportions of the houses, streets and squares are in themselves urbanistic achievements which should be preserved for the sake of their harmonious character and for the happiness that they bring to the *human being*.

This leads me to the fourth factor: the *economic* one. The architectural heritage is a non-renewable asset and it must be made to bear fruit in the same way as the soil which sustains our agriculture or the factories which keep our industries alive. Any deterioration suffered by this heritage is a national impoverishment. The cultural heritage is not a luxury. It is an integral part of the national economy. Of course, one of the best examples of this is the economic contribution of monuments and sites to the tourist trade. The experts of the Organization for Economic Cooperation and Development, which is based in Paris, have calculated the part played by tourism in the general economy of a country. For many states these figures reveal that tourism is a leading industry and one of the main sources of employment and revenue. By letting the monuments deteriorate and also by spoiling the landscape or the coastline, we are killing the goose that lays the golden egg.

Facts such as these compel us to act. What action do we propose to take? There are several answers to this very difficult question. The first and most obvious is to educate and rouse public opinion. This is the main concern of all the voluntary organizations of which this country can be so justly proud and of which most are represented here today. We must always remember that there is no hope for political action unless there is strong public demand and support. Our first duty is to encourage children at school to understand and respect their cultural heritage. A child today will be a mayor tomorrow, a member of parliament, or a minister, or an architect, thus he will be responsible at some level for action to be taken either for or against our inheritance, in stone. If he has not been trained and prepared to assume this responsibility, how can we expect him to act wisely in a field where so much wisdom is required? Architecture must be shown to children as something which *is* living, which *has* lived in the past, which *must* live in the future, and which they themselves are responsible for keeping alive. Of course, this education of public opinion should go far beyond childhood. The architectural heritage should also form part of secondary and university education. Special emphasis should be laid on extra-mural and adult education, which nowadays reaches so many people. In connection with this policy, the possibilities of television, films, broadcasting and the press, should be constantly explored, either to protest against the harm which is done or to applaud the successes which are achieved. I would like at this stage to pay a very special tribute to the *Scottish Civic Trust* and to the *National*

16. Ann Street, Edinburgh

17. A New York office canyon

Trust for Scotland. They are represented here today at this conference. For many years they have devoted all their efforts to the cause of arousing public interest in your vernacular architecture. But there is, of course, a limit to what can be achieved by private enterprise. Nowadays the problems have become so great that, more often than not, they must be solved at a local government, or at a regional, or state, level. In some cases, this inheritance is the sole responsibility of cities, or of *Länder* (as in Germany and Austria), or *Cantons*, as in Switzerland. Most countries are becoming increasingly aware of this responsibility and are setting up specialized departments to deal with these matters. Hence the need for new legislation adapted to the problems of our time as well as for specialized administrations and (of course) for more money.

At this level it is essential for governments to know exactly how to face the problems and how other countries are facing them. This is precisely the type of cooperation which has been recommended by a recent conference of ministers: European ministers especially responsible for sites and monuments, at a conference which was convened, in November last, in Brussels. At a European level the ministers have made three separate recommendations. *First*, the heads of the departments, in our member states, responsible for preservation of monuments and sites and for town and country planning, respectively, should meet regularly to examine whatever problems they might have in common. You may know that for the last five years, this has already been arranged on an *ad hoc* basis within the framework of the Council of Europe. One of these meetings, which was attended by several among you, was held at Bath three years ago, when Professor Buchanan was one of the speakers. But the main difference between these meetings and those advocated by the ministers at the recent conference in Brussels is that, in future, governmental experts specializing in the protection of the cultural heritage of monuments and sites will meet together with governmental experts specializing in town and country planning. Thus, for the first time in Europe, cooperation will be instituted between different government departments whose actions ought to be complementary. Public opinion will be represented on this committee, which is about to come into being, by members of the Consultative Assembly of the Council of Europe and of the European Conference of Local Authorities, and also by representatives of such European non-governmental organizations as *Europa Nostra*.

The *second* recommendation by the ministers for international action is the preparation of a *charter*. This charter would embody the principles which I have just underlined, and would serve as a basic document for action. The elements of this charter would probably be based on the conclusions of the ministers in Brussels, in the terms of a report now being drafted by a team of Europeans, chaired by M. François Sorlin. This charter, it is hoped, will lead one day to some sort of international legal instrument, binding upon European governments.

The *third* recommendation is the preparation of an 'International Year' devoted to the preservation of the cultural heritage of monuments and sites. This Year is likely to be held in 1974, and would have the aims of making Europeans aware of the danger to their common heritage and of integrating the culture of the past into the society of today and of tomorrow. The success of European Conservation Year has encouraged us to prepare the *Monuments and Sites Year* for which every effort, both governmental and non-governmental, should be mobilized.

I would like at this point to add a note of encouragement and hope for the future. I am certain that the revival of interest in our architectural inheritance, which we witness around us in all our countries, is the expression of a strong and growing need. Should I wish to have some assurance in this respect, I need only look at the various long-term plans which are at present going forward in Europe. In reading the document of this conference on Georgian Edinburgh I was struck by the emphasis laid on long-term action. A twenty-year plan, in our days of rapid change, is indeed an expression of a high degree of confidence in the future.

This is my first visit to Edinburgh and it fulfils a dream I have had for a long time of coming here; so I cannot speak in terms of real assessment or knowledge of what is going on here, what is the dimension of the problem and what are the real means necessary. But the little I have seen has struck me and impressed me beyond any expectation I might have had. Of course for me, as for all Europeans, Edinburgh is one of the outstanding epitomes of culture and of beauty. But precisely because it is, for all of us in Europe, so identified with the criteria of culture, of beauty, one tends to take it for granted that Edinburgh will forever remain the embodiment of these values. Thus, to come to this city and to see and be told and be shown proof of the immense scale and complexity of the problems and dangers confronting this city is something that comes really as a shock. It is just not possible to imagine that Edinburgh might lose, that Britain, that Europe, might lose this immense asset. It is just as incredible as thinking that Venice may be swallowed up by its lagoon — which alas is a real and tragic possibility. But, as I said at the beginning, the sheer size of the audience and the importance of the personalities and national organizations mobilized here today are in themselves a great guarantee, and I firmly believe that the work undertaken here will set an example for Europe. That such enthusiasm can be aroused is an augury of success. I wish to tell you all how keenly the Council of

Europe supports this action and convey to you the best wishes of this European intergovernmental organization. The Council of Europe wishes every success to this Conference and the achievement of the work undertaken for the restoration of Georgian Edinburgh.

The Conservation of Georgian Edinburgh

The Stones of Edinburgh

When I come into Edinburgh I am in the capital of another country. *19*
I recognize the fact even from the architecture, for the architecture of
Scotland is most triumphant. Now the architects of Scotland have had
more influence on the architecture of England almost than the English
architects themselves. I think of Sir William Chambers—of the house
(now the Royal Bank) he built in St Andrew's Square, but also of his
Somerset House in the Strand; of the Adam brothers, who are famous all
over the world—and how splendid Robert's Register House looks today;
of Gibbs, that earlier architect who brought baroque to Britain and
designed the Radcliffe Camera, St Martin's-in-the-Fields, St Mary-le-
Strand, and the Fellows Building at King's, Cambridge; of Telford as
an architect and engineer; the Rennies, both father and son. And then
to go on to more recent Scottish architects who have influenced not just
England but the whole world—George Walton, Rennie Mackintosh,
Lorimer, and to me the greatest church architect who died only recently,
the Aberdonian Sir Ninian Comper. These are great architects, and they
are Scottish, or from Scotland. But the mighty men who laid out the New
Town and went on in Edinburgh afterwards—Playfair, Gillespie, Elliot,
Burn—they are unknown to English people. And other towns in Scotland have their equivalents to these men: 'Greek' Thomson in Glasgow,

18. Classical Edinburgh
19. National Gallery and Edinburgh Castle, drawn by Playfair

20. Georgian buildings in Perth

20 Archibald Simpson in Aberdeen, and whoever was responsible for the
marvellous Georgian work in places like Perth.

21 That architectural quality of Scotland is deeply impressive, and here,
in its heart, the New Town is the most important of all because here you
get the greatest extent of it.

I notice one quality in Scottish buildings, whether in the New Town
or the old—that marvellous contrast—and that is, it's nearly always
more three-dimensional than architecture in Ireland, for instance, where
you get a splendid facade, but it's rather thin behind. In Italy you often
find this stage scenery effect, and in France too, particularly in the
baroque period. But in Scotland, even if you're being Greek, you usually
carry the design round all sides of a building. Take the backs of Randolph

22 Crescent, Ainslie Place, Moray Place, as seen from across the Dean
Bridge; or Buccleuch Place from the Meadows! And when you go *into*
a building—even though it was built as what you call *flats*—the staircases, the ironwork of the staircases, and the handrails—these are
things to grasp as well as decoration. In Scotland a house which looks
rather simple outside is very often grand inside.

We had mention of Bath. The city of Bath is not like that. It is a grand
facade, and its grandest facade of all, Royal Crescent, was built *as a*

21. Charlotte Square, Edinburgh

22. Randolph Crescent from Eton Terrace, Edinburgh

facade. The houses were filled in behind it and were built for people to live in during the season. But the quality of Scottish architecture is *23, 24*   thorough—through and through; beautiful ironwork, beautiful moulding, detail wherever you look.

23. The Royal Bank, St Andrew's Square, Edinburgh

24. Reconstruction in the Canongate, Edinburgh

25   And didn't they understand skylines! Edinburgh is visual delight to the walker. Wherever you look, country suddenly appears at the end of a street; or an outline has been contrived like that of Playfair's St Stephen's Church down there; or the Adam church over there; or Melville Column *out* there; or the outline of the Old Town and the Castle and Salisbury Crags. There is a last point I want to make.

So Edinburgh is what a city ought to be (or could be), somewhere to live and walk about in. Old towns were originally built on hilltops for the double purpose of protection from man as enemy and from the bad weather, another formidable foe. This was mediaeval, seventeenth century.

In the eighteenth century, they were planned in the grand way of the New Town—for carriage folks as well as for pedestrians—how well it was done. Recently Sir Leslie Martin, Professor of Architecture at Cambridge, went over to New York and looked at high buildings there, to try and find out what was the best way to get as many people as possible onto a given space. He discovered that the way to do this was not, as we fondly imagine, by building tall slabs which have terrific draughts between them and have to be far apart in order that there may be day light on the ground floor of the next slab—and what's called open space: a sort of arid recce ground with litter all over it. No, he found one can fit most people onto land by building in *squares*—not more than eight storeys high, with service roads at the back and the quiet in the middle. So James Craig was well ahead of his time, in 1767!

Scotland has always been a place for people with long heads who could see into the future. We know that the policy of destruction is old fashioned and retrogressive. We know too that to build in squares, as they did in the New Town, is a sensible way to build. So the New Town will be saved. I hope that I have shown that it is unneccessary to speak on its behalf: the New Town speaks for itself.

25. Edinburgh, from the north

COLIN BUCHANAN

The Case for Conservation

What has struck me about everything that has so far been said is that
the case for conservation of the New Town has not been questioned at all.
There seems to be an absolute unquestioned assumption that the New
Town should be conserved. Now, you have got to make some allowances
for me because I have gone through, recently, a soul-searching experience
in the hard school of Mr Justice Roskill's commission on the third London
Airport. In the rigorous intellectual atmosphere of that academy (which
I think is going to blow a wind through planning thought in this country
in the next few years) I can tell you that an assumption that the New
Town should be conserved would not pass unquestioned for one moment.
It would be taken to pieces detail by detail and justification demanded at
every step. Now, please do not get me wrong. I have said enough to be
got seriously wrong already, but don't get me wrong, don't assume that
I am saying there is *no* case for the conservation of the New Town
because I am not. I am saying that there are pros and cons for conservation. Or, to use the contemporary term, there are costs and benefits to be
attached to any process of conservation. This must be so, I think you will
agree.

Obviously, one could argue a case *against* conservation. With what I
have learnt in the last two years I could stand up now and argue a case
against the conservation of the New Town, and I would base it on the
value of the opportunities which conservation, because it freezes the
physical fabric of a large area, would cause to be permanently lost to
the community. Now, so far, to the best of my knowledge, no attempt
has been made to undertake a cost/benefit study in respect of proposals
for conserving the building fabric of an area of a town. We certainly
did not attempt this, my partners and I, in the study that we undertook
for the conservation of part of Bath. I think one can explain this, probably,
by the fact that this cost/benefit analysis is a new analytical tool. It is
very new, it is relatively untried, and I doubt whether anyone at the
present time really knows enough to be able to attribute values—reliable
values—to the many items that would have to be brought into the
account; but my guess is that it is not going to be very long before we
do apply this technique to such matters as conservation, if for no other
reason than to sort out priorities as between various claims on our capital
resources. When we come to do this there may be some shocks in store
for us and some time-honoured values and attitudes may be found, in
fact, to be unrelated to the needs of contemporary life. But we are not

26. Warriston Crescent, Edinburgh

there yet, and meanwhile you in Edinburgh have nailed your flag to the mast as far as the conservation of the New Town is concerned. I am pretty certain, for reasons I have given, that one of these fine days you may be arraigned for this and brought before some high tribunal of cost/benefit analysts. And you will be asked to justify your procedures. You may have quite a tough time defending yourselves but my forecast is that in the end you will present a case so convincing that you will be honourably acquitted.

I am not going to try to argue your case for you—that is being done effectively by others. I merely want to say this: from experience of having wandered around a good deal of the world in the last few years, having seen urban environments that overpower, others that terrify, some that revolt you for their ostentatiousness, and some that wring the heart for their meanness and poverty, I really have no doubt whatsoever of the wisdom of preserving this suave, gentle, restrained collection of houses *26* and streets, terraces and squares and gardens, that you have here in the New Town and which beyond any argument, I think, is one of the best things to be found in the urban areas of the world. But I think I am giving you good advice in suggesting that you do turn your thoughts in the direction of analyzing the costs and the benefits of conservation.

D*

Not merely to forearm yourselves against an onslaught that may be made one day, but also because I think you could find things to your own advantage in the sense that the costs of conservation can, over time, be offset by substantial benefits. I have a picture in my mind's eye of the report of this hypothetical cost/benefit analysis. I can see that it might be called a *value*, to the nation, of the New Town of Edinburgh. I think you could present the New Town as one of the main cultural assets of the Nation, high up on the list, and put it in a way that Government would find it very difficult not to support and at the same time I dare say, you know, that you could present the accounts in a way that would bring the costs over time into perspective and make them seem a good deal less formidable than they appear in the Report (*see* appendix).

I turn to another aspect. I think it has been made fairly plain that this Conference is primarily concerned with the maintenance of the fabric of the New Town. I do not want to stray outside the terms of reference of the Conference, but it may be expected of me that I should refer briefly to the work which I and my partners are undertaking in Edinburgh along with Messrs Freeman Fox Wilbur Smith & Associates. Our terms of reference in this study, which we are now up to the neck in, are to recommend a transport plan for the central area of Edinburgh which will achieve high standards of accessibility by public and private transport and yet be compatible—and this is the nub of it—with the retention and enhancement of the City's architectural and landscape heritage. That is the real point, and the whole of the New Town falls fairly and squarely in the area we are studying. But, you may ask, what has traffic got to do with conservation?

There are two points which I would like to emphasize: first, and this is directly relevant to the preservation of the fabric in the sense with which this Conference is concerned, there is damage done to paintwork and to stonework by pollution from vehicle fumes and there is damage to the structure of the buildings as a result of vibration from traffic. Now, I don't know—and I question whether anyone really knows—how far the present state of decay is due to these two particular causes. It may be that one could exaggerate, but nevertheless there must be some connection, and so my advice here would be—don't just be content with rectifying the damage to buildings from these causes, but seek also to tackle those causes at root. In other words, batter away for all you are worth for the better control of vehicle fumes and for the routing of· heavy vehicles away from the areas of great architectural value. I think that is directly relevant to the subject of the Conference.

My second point is indirect. I think you will find in the last analysis that the most certain way to ensure the conservation of buildings of

27

27. A build-up of traffic in a central Edinburgh street

architectural value is to ensure that they are occupied by people who will cherish them. I think this is what you should be aiming at and I suggest this could be a surer base than, say, trying to enforce conservation on occupiers or owners who are not really interested and who could not be relied upon to maintain improvements that might be made.

There are a number of factors that bear on this question of getting a state of affairs where the buildings are occupied by people likely to cherish them. One of the most important of these, I think, is traffic. Take the New Town itself. If it is your view, for example, that it is greatly to be desired that this should be mainly occupied by people who love the buildings, then it needs to be made into a place that these same people are likely to be attracted to to live in and this in turn means, I think, that it should not be so infested with traffic that it is ugly, noisy, ridden with fumes, and maybe downright dangerous. In the work we are doing in Edinburgh, it is a major preoccupation of ours to see how the traffic in the New Town can be kept under control, not just now, but in the future against the tide of rising car ownership, and maintained at volumes that are compatible with that splendid environment. This is an important aspect of conservation. But of course there is another side of it. There's the love/hate relationship.

I believe that one of the attributes that will contribute to making the new Town liveable is that the residents themselves should have reasonable freedom to use their cars and to keep them in the locality. I myself see no way of avoiding this. I think it is one thing to say, 'keep the commuters off parking all over the streets of the New Town', but I think it is another to say, 'bar the residents from having cars', though I dare say the pressure could be applied gently and gradually to get them to arrange parking for themselves off the streets. The other side of it is, of course, that traffic, I am afraid, cannot just be expunged from an area. You cannot just make it disappear into thin air. I have been searching for ten years for some method of making exactly that happen; regretfuly I have come to the conclusion that it cannot be done. Some of it you can expunge but a good deal has got to be provided with some other route. I can't, I am afraid, give any guarantee that we won't be involved in something of this kind in Edinburgh which is going to involve some people somewhere in (alas) what to them will be agonizing. I wish I could see a way of avoiding that. But to enter on that subject would be to go right outside the terms of reference.

I can conclude however that it would be a mistake to rely entirely upon traffic being dealt with by measures from above, as it were. That is to say, by regulations, by orders, by the building of parking structures, by the building of new roads, and so on. The more I look round, the more

I am convinced that a great deal could be achieved in the way of com-
batting some of these unpleasant effects of traffic, simply and solely by
improved behaviour and restraint in the use of vehicles. I think we
could get a major improvement almost for nothing.

Let me end on an encouraging note. When we started work on the traffic
problems of Edinburgh, one of the first things we did was to ask for
suggestions from the public and in particular we invited answers to a
number of questions including one relating to the use of private cars in
the central area of the City. It's true that the answers we received
represented only a very small sample of the population of the City, but
nevertheless it was gratifying to observe the number of people who
seemed acutely aware of the conflict between traffic and the character of
the central environment, and the proportion who went further than that
and said that they would be prepared to accept some restraint on the use
of private vehicles if by doing they could help to protect the character of
the City. That seemed to us to indicate a very responsible attitude, but
perhaps it was only what we ought to have expected from the inheritors
of the New Town.

28. Traffic in Edinburgh in 1885

SIR ROBERT MATTHEW

The State of the Fabric

It is my task to present a survey of buildings in the New Town, organized
on behalf of the Civic Trust for Scotland by The Edinburgh Architectural
Association, along with recommendations dealing with the maintenance
of the fabric. The Report, reprinted as an appendix, gives a history of
the building of the various sections of the New Town. It describes the
nature of the survey and the kind of assessments made on the facts
thereby presented. It gives an estimate of probable costs likely to be
incurred in maintaining the buildings in good condition and finally it
indicates a possible organization that might be adopted to deal with a
continuing policy of repairs and restorations.

In the Report we have emphasized that the survey of the fabric is
only a start. The basic facts, as they are today, are one chapter in a
dramatic story that began two hundred years ago. The story goes on,
but nothing remains static. It is with the effects of use and weather on
mainly stone buildings that we are, in this particular chapter, prin-
cipally concerned. Underlying all this, however, is a basic assumption:
an assumption that many of us (and I include myself) have taken for
granted for much too long without realizing its implications. The
assumption is simply this: that the New Town of Edinburgh, in the
broad terms in which we have defined it, stands by the severest architectural and environmental standards in the highest class of world-wide
examples. Let us remember that there are not, after all, so very many of
these. This in fact is the foundation of our case. As a citizen of Edinburgh,
like many of you here, I myself may be somewhat biased by my own
long associations and I am not going to elaborate this argument. I believe
it is recognized by all those whose judgement in these matters is to be
respected. Not least, by the City authorities whose views are set out in
their Development Plan review of 1965, and more recently as indicated
by their extensive work on the conservation areas. Their views are well
known. In fact, almost the whole argument for our case today can be
deduced from two statements to be found in the Conservation Report by
the City Town Planning Department on *Zone One* — a central zone representing an area about one-fifth of the total ground surveyed for this
conference. *Map no 16* in that Conservation Report shows those buildings
in the zone classed as of architectural and historic interest. Nearly *all*
the buildings throughout the zone are classed as buildings of national
importance, buildings of *Category A*. A remarkable consistency of
excellence, extending as it does from west to east for more than a mile.

That is the first statement. The second one, however, is equally important. Commenting on the condition of the fabric come these ominous words, and I quote: 'None of the buildings according to structural condition can be classified on account of their age in what would normally be the best category of buildings'. And it goes on to describe the principal ways in which deterioration has set in. Here, we have it in a nutshell. Architecturally, the finest quality on a world-scale; but as to condition, quite a different story.

Our survey took about a year to carry through. It represented I do not know how many man-hours of solid work in all weathers under the guidance of Mr John Reid. There was no lack of volunteers. In addition, by courtesy of the University of Edinburgh, there was access to a computer, making possible, not only now but I hope also in the future, rapid estimates of cost allocations in relation to various building elements such as stonework, chimneys, roof, ironwork, and so on. Almost completely, there was cooperation from householders. I sympathize quite a bit with those, for I am one myself, occupying part of 'a national treasure'—I quote the words used by Colin Buchanan in his report at Bath. They; we; at any rate our buildings, will no doubt be subjected to much scrutiny in the years to come and I hope that you—we—will bear with it with some sympathy and not be tempted to take the extreme view, which I have heard on only two occasions during the whole of this operation, that these fact-finding missions somehow imply a threat to private property. If any of you have been unduly disturbed during the survey, I regret it, but on behalf of the survey teams, I here record my appreciation of the general tolerance (and much more) extended to all of us during these past months.

The question has sometimes been put: surely the condition of fabric is only one part of a total problem, a problem including use of buildings, open spaces, traffic, parking, rating, licensing, and so on? This, of course, is perfectly true, but we have been explicit that these wider aspects of conservation have been outside our terms of reference. We are in this matter, and for this Conference, merely an aid to the City. We are armed with all the apparatus, legal and administrative, of the Town Planning process. On this platform today, along with the Lord Provost and the Chairman of the Planning Committee, are Lord Holford and Mr Colin Buchanan, both deeply involved on behalf of the City, in their various ways, in these wider problems. Our task today is to focus on one aspect of the New Town, a fundamental one, we believe, involving a possible financial commitment that the normal provisions of the statutes and the resources of private owners are unlikely to provide for. We are asking in fact for special consideration for this national treasure; an argument that can be justified only by the most exceptional circumstances. All those involved in the future of Edinburgh are aware of this problem. But the spelling out of the case in detail has to be done, to help convince all those concerned, not least those responsible for eking out the limited resources of the national purse.

I propose, therefore, to illustrate something of the scale, the character, the dignity of the *New Town*. But, first, to relate these pictures to their environment—to the Old Town as it was until the 1750s, and to the City as it exists today—let us look at a short series of plans. The first shows Edinburgh about 1750, the Old Town on the crag-and-tail ridge running east from the castle rock, with open fields to the north where the New Town was to arise. Next we have James Craig's first plan (1767) of the New Town. It was described correctly, I think, by Professor Youngson, as a very modest plan involving no great ideas of town planning. The site was the area immediately north of the loch (now Princes Street Gardens) and the scale was roughly just under a mile from east to west, and about a third of a mile from north to south. Within fifty years, however, the town had grown considerably, as can be observed from a plan of 1820. Most of the New Town was in fact there. Next, we show the famous cast-

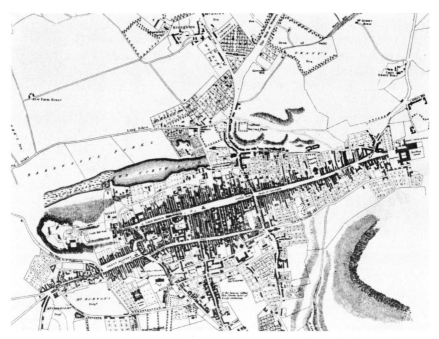

29. Edinburgh about 1750. The open country to the north of the loch is the site of the New Town

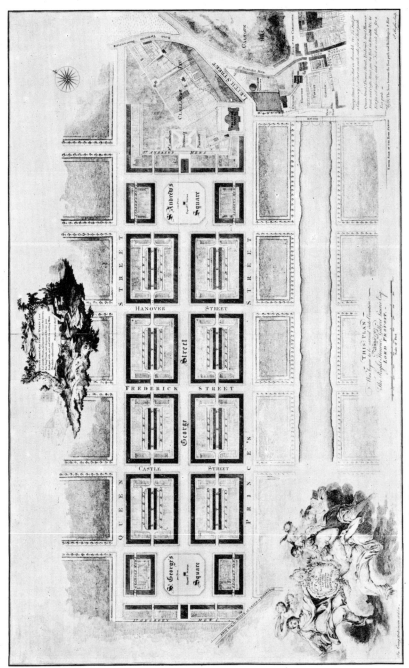

30. James Craig's plan (1767) of the New Town

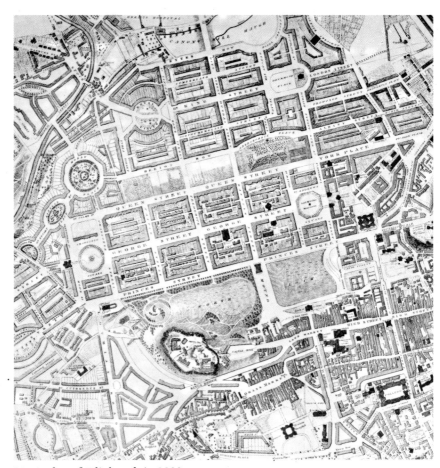

31. A plan of Edinburgh in 1820

iron model first illustrated in Professor Youngson's *Classical Edinburgh*.
It shows, very vividly, the relative size of the old town of Edinburgh,
compared to the New Town itself. The New Town very quickly trebled the
total size of the city.

31, 32

    The next set of plans show, first the survey area, in black, in relation to
the main central parts of the town. It's a very large area indeed. For the
purposes of the study, this survey area was divided into seven zones,
plus an eighth peripheral one. Teams were organized on a zonal basis.
The four special areas shown were selected by the (English) Department
for Special Study (and the *Kennet* Report was a consequence of the
coordination of these four towns). You can see that all these four can be
put within the New Town area, with some ground to spare.

33-36

32. Cast-iron model of Edinburgh about 1820

I shall now try and take you on a brief guided tour through the New   *37-44*
Town, showing, first, some of the great set pieces, and then selecting a
few individual buildings which come as incidents in the scene.

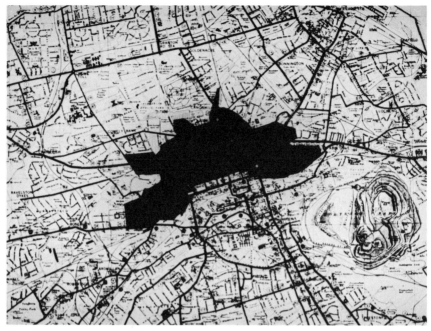

33. The survey area, in black

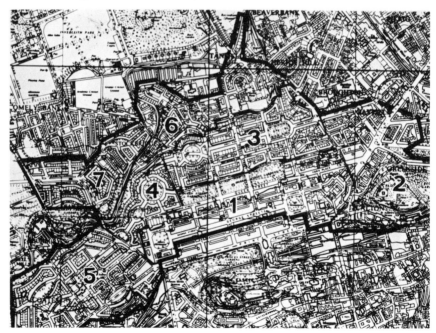

34. The divisions of the survey area

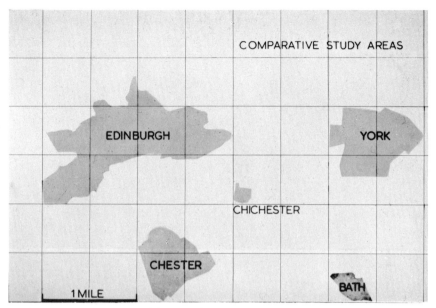

35. The comparative size of four English study areas

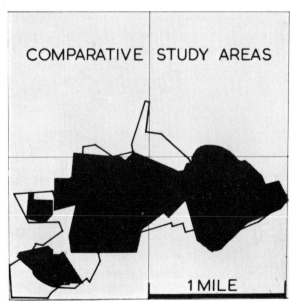

36. The four study areas in plate 35 superimposed on the Edinburgh survey area

37. Burns' monument and Arthur's Seat

38. Waterloo Place and Calton Hill

39. Register House, about 1780 (Robert Adam)

40. Heriot Row, 1803 (Robert Reid)

41. Moray Place, about 1825 (Gillespie Graham)

42. The house in North Castle Street where Sir Walter Scott lived from 1802–26

43. Wm Blackwood's shop, George Street.   44. Ann Street, central block

Thirty years ago, a small group of post-graduate architectural students carried out a town-planning survey and study of the City as a whole, illustrated by an exhibition held in the Royal Scottish Academy. Part of that study was a detailed analysis of the New Town and the way in which the grand plans broke down, trailing away at the edges in the middle of the nineteenth century. Reading over that study recently and examining the plans, I was much struck by the fact that the state of the fabric at that time received no mention at all. Looking back, I do not remember (because I was part of that student group) being impressed in any way with the deterioration of the stone. Maybe the past thirty years have seen an acceleration of a process that must have started well before that. I do not know, I don't recall any general reports on the matter, except, occasionally, the late Principal Smail writing to *The Scotsman* about it. Then, about five years ago, the architectural members of the *Fine Art Commission for Scotland* had occasion to look closely at various parts of the New Town. One and all, we were dismayed by what we saw.

It was not only at the fringes, where some properties, even some streets, had gone almost past the point of repair, that there was cause for concern. Throughout the terraces, the squares and the crescents, even to the most prominent and distinguished of all, time and atmosphere had clearly brought alarming changes. In some cases, repairs through the years had been carried out—in a few cases, well carried out. For the most part,

45 however, processes of erosion and decay were proceeding without effective intervention. Sometimes, indeed, action had been taken (probably on account of safety) with quite bizarre effects. I am not speaking here of structural stability. With very few exceptions, the principal

46 structures seem to be sound. There is one exception, however. Chimneys, for a long time, have been a source of concern and the skylines, to which the massive chimney walls contributed, and were intended to contribute, so much character, present today a sad and shabby top and finish to the elegant buildings below. Many of the stone stacks have been covered in cement, sometimes replaced by crude red brickwork, singularly out of character in this context. But by far the most serious problems arise with cornices, columns, balasters, string courses, window architraves, balustrades, pediments, indeed, with all these finely-carved architectural details on which so much of the outstanding quality of the New Town depends. The popular notion that the New Town, by being built of Craigleith stone, legendary for its wearing quality, could indefinitely defy the weather, is alas far from the truth. When it is found, Craigleith is today in pretty good shape; but in striking contrast are the many softer stones brought from different quarries, often found side by side with the enduring Craigleith. As a result, mouldings, particularly those

heavily undercut like the main cornices, are flaking away, sometimes dangerously, and when this goes too far—as it has already in many places—the temptation is simply to shave away the decorative features down to the main face of the building and leave it at that. In a few instances cemented imitations have already replaced the original delicate *47* detail. In addition to this, some of the main front walls, probably laid against the natural stone bed, are themselves flaking, as gravestones are apt to do when they are standing on end. This has been going on for quite a long time, as a close examination will reveal. To use a good Scottish building expression, *'clouring away and slaistering'*, that is, *48* cutting back with an iron claw and then cementing up to a fair surface, 'clouring away and slaistering', is widespread. The next stage to that, inevitably, is painting the stone, and at that point the essential character *49, 50* of the buildings of the New Town will have gone for ever.

I have spoken so far about the problems of stone. From the point of view of total costs, it is of course the heaviest item by a long way. It is not, however, the whole story by any means. In order to carry out the survey in the single year we allowed ourselves, we had to confine it to the exteriors of the buildings. We do not know, therefore, the possible extent of *internal* deterioration, or its distribution. Some information on internal conditions is known to the City *Town Planning Department*, in relation to the conservation zones already surveyed. Relying mainly on records for improvement grants already made, and also on information from firms who have undertaken remedial work, it is known, for instance, that most buildings in the New Town were built without damp-proof courses. Most basements are probably affected to some extent by rising damp, and some in fact have been closed under exceptional circumstances by the Public Health Department. None of these factors have been covered by the present survey.

The principal problems classified in the survey in addition to the stone-work are as follows. First, what we have called *roof issues*—a telling *52* phrase. That is, the multitude of defects arising in gulleys, valleys, flat roofs, ridges and rones, chimneyheads, in fact roof junctions of all kinds, as well as the conditions of the main roof-coverings themselves. Then *doors and windows*: the special problems of replacing astragals, decorated *51* fanlights, and the doors themselves. You see some very strange doors. Then, *below-ground areas*: entrance steps and platforms, a great problem on the sloping sites where they are cutting into the ground, sometimes causing great trouble with penetration of water. Then *railings*: these need little underlining.

My next section, therefore, is an attempt to illustrate these various aspects.

45. General decay

46. Cement chimneyhead

47. False methods of restoration

48. *Clouring away and slaistering*

49. Painting of stone

50. Painting of stone

51. Erosion of window consols

52. Destruction of balasters

Our survey, then, has confirmed the concern felt by many as to the future. Where do we go from here? Before coming to the recommendations for action, I should say a few words about the assessment (given in the Report) of costs of restoration. When we started this operation, I think it is fair to say that no-one had any real notion about total costs in relation to the whole of the New Town. The City conservation reports on Zones 1 and 5, already published, had given some indication for these areas, taken on a sample basis. Apart from this, we really had nothing. We are indebted to the surveyor members of the survey teams for the information upon which is based the assessment of costs set out in the Report. We are particularly indebted to Mr Ian Ramsay from the University, who has coordinated this part of the report and has kept the computer busy.

I would like to emphasize the cautionary explanations given on costs. The basis of costing has been undertaken not on individual occupancies but on a broader unit of size. This unit of size, depending on the nature of the particular architectural composition of the street, on how it had been designed and built, might be a single building or a whole terrace. For this reason—and I underline this—costs for any single property cannot be assessed by interpolating from the figures given. These are merely averages, and the relative costs for single properties could vary either up or down.

The overall assessment gives total costs for all categories of repairs, in relation to each of the survey sub-divisions which I have already mentioned. Naturally, both the totals and the averages vary considerably. The breakdown of the averages, in relation to building elements, very clearly indicates the predominant problem everywhere—that of stone repairing and cleaning; this accounts for over sixty-seven per cent of the total averages. Adding up all the areas, the total cost comes to about £8·5m. You could compare this with the total gross annual value, that is, a reasonable assessment of total rents, for all properties of about £1·75m. On the assumptions that these total figures are a fair indication of the order of costs likely to be involved, and that there will be general agreement that an active policy of repair and restoration should, and can, be carried through, two sets of questions then arise. First, under what circumstances can a practical policy for repair and restoration be established, involving both the setting of standards as to what kind of work should be done and, second, an assurance that such standards can be maintained through the years. Second, how can the necessary costs be met, and by whom?

The recommendations of the Report refer to both these sets of questions. The initial recommendation is that a *New Town Advisory Committee* should be immediately set up, and I quote, 'to advise the appropriate authorities on the measures necessary to maintain the New Town'. Such a committee would not in any way supersede the planning functions of the Coporation, but it would represent the principal interests involved, namely the Corporation, the *Historic Buildings Council, The Cockburn Association, The National Trust for Scotland, The Scottish Civic Trust*, and the *Scottish Georgian Society*, and we suggest it would have, in addition, two independent members, representing property owners and occupiers; and that it would also have power to co-opt if necessary. The first task of this Committee would be to establish a set of building and architectural standards to which all proposals, for repairs and restoration work, would be referred. The Committee would collaborate with street associations in setting up a series of what we have called *street schemes*. The general scope of such a street scheme is set out in the Report. I would draw your attention to one paragraph. 'It will be important to encourage existing New Town street associations and to help form others, where they do not presently exist.'

These associations would be of great value in creating the climate in which owners would be encouraged to make improvements to their property and to undertake, possibly on a community basis, further surveys of the property in their streets. In a similar way, societies with expert knowledge like the *Georgian*, the *Cockburn*, could obviously be of the very greatest help. I would not minimize the amount of work likely to be involved. We are starting an operation of great magnitude. The total number of properties is very large, much larger than anything so far tackled in this country. The Committee will need to be adequately staffed and professionally advised, but it has been assumed that once the thing gets off the ground, time programmes will be planned, covering, say, five year periods; and priorities set, in order to avoid an unmanageable flood of work at the beginning.

As to finance, we start with a large probable expenditure ahead. £8·5m is a lot of money. On the other hand, in relation to the total number of properties and to a reasonable time-scale for actual spending, it is not astronomical. When we come to individual cases, however, and the capacity of individual property owners to face the cost of repairs, there is bound, in the very nature of things, to be a very wide variety of circumstance. Structural conditions do not necessarily bear direct relation to types of ownership or indeed even to the use of the buildings. We have set out various possibilities for sharing costs between owners, town council, and government. The Report gives an example—and I emphasize it is only an example—of a sharing by the Historic Buildings Council of 50 per cent, local authority of 25 per cent and property owner of 25 per cent. A total figure of £15m, in place of the £8·5m, has been assessed as a fair allowance to meet probable increases in building costs—we have said *probable*, but I would say *certain*—over a period of, say, 20 years. This, again, is taken as an assumed minimum time necessary to overtake the whole of this task. On a $50\% + 25\% + 25\%$ basis, and assuming a more or less even flow of work year by year, the Historic Buildings Council would then have to pay out, annually, £375,000, local authority, £187,000; and all the owners together, another £187,000. An annual total of £0·75m for 20 years, while not astronomical, is clearly outside (and I would say in many cases, well outside) the normal range of finance available through grants of one kind or another for architectural and historic buildings, however distinguished these may be. To give you an idea of the order of spending needed, the total annual budget for 1968–69 for the Historic Buildings Council for the whole of Scotland was in the region of only £80,000. Under our computation they would have to pay at least twice that for the *one* case of Edinburgh. In this special situation, the major financial participation arrangements must be worked out primarily between the Government and the local authority. That would probably be the first thing the Committee would have to initiate. We have noted that it is very unlikely that a blanket scheme of non-contributory grants would be acceptable to the authorities. Whatever financial arrangements are ultimately made, the scheme will have to be sufficiently flexible to meet a very wide variety of need. Finally, we have felt it desirable, partly for obvious reasons, partly to point out the exceptional nature of the problem, to suggest raising a fund on a United Kingdom basis, as a *revolving fund* to be used for loans, purchase, restoration and re-sale. We have put a figure there of £0·5m.

There, then, is the outline of the case. We feel we now have sufficient physical evidence to justify exceptional measures. We have sketched out a possible course of action for the purpose of discussion. We do not minimize the difficulties inherent in mounting the kind and scale of operation which we can see is necessary. Not least of these is the need to mobilize an effective body of opinion in support.

Let me sum up. We have assumed that the New Town is recognized as an area of outstanding value, on both a national and an international scale of values. We have argued that for this reason it merits special consideration, both administratively and financially, by the responsible authorities. The survey just carried out has confirmed the need for exceptional measures, starting as soon as possible and spread over a reasonable number of years, for the preservation of the physical fabric of the New Town buildings. Total costs as we have computed them will be high but not beyond contemplation. There can be no case for writing off the New Town as a crumbling relic on that account. At the same time it is certain that in many cases costs of adequate restoration will be clearly beyond normal means available, either by the City or by individual owners. It is in fact to the Government that we must turn. This is the message we wish to put across. We suggest an immediate and simple piece of machinery to make the next move to begin this great operation. Let us remember that with every year that passes, something literally rubs off the buildings and is lost. With every year, too, costs of restoring the fabric increase steadily. If what we have said is true, if what we have put forward can be accepted, then a progressive investment will be put into the New Town that I believe the most prudent of economists would (with their hands on their hearts, if not on their purse-strings) unquestionably approve.

A. J. YOUNGSON

The Cost of Civilization

As a mere economist, I speak with some diffidence, although that is not regarded as a leading characteristic of economists. Also, I should like to speak to a text, although the connections between economics and the Church are not usually thought of as particularly close. And just to muddle things up a little further, the text I have chosen is not from the Bible, but from Shakespeare, who wrote:

Why so large cost having so short a lease

Dost thou upon thy fading mansion spend?

Finally, I have to admit that in these lines Shakespeare is apparently referring, not to the building trade but to the cosmetics business. As an economist I feel free to ignore a literary detail. I want to say something about the Case *for* conservation, for, as Colin Buchanan said, not anything very much has been said about it; and one has to face the fact that there are many people, many in influential positions who (to put it no more strongly) are rather indifferent to propositions of this sort. If conservation cost nothing, there would be no difficulty. But conservation does cost something, and therefore there is opposition and it is on these two points that I want to speak.

Why should we want to conserve the New Town; why should we want to conserve the Parthenon? The answer is at once quite simple and extremely difficult to state. We want to conserve these artefacts because they are important expressions of civilization. Civilization comes and goes; and not many, I imagine, would venture to say that in our time we have any too much of it. The New Town of Edinburgh is one of the great products — or rather is the product — of one of the great ages of civilization, namely the Enlightenment, in which Scotland and Scotsmen played a particularly distinguished part. The New Town in its order, in the excellence of its proportions, in its marvellous combining of the built with the unbuilt environment: in all these ways the New Town is a superlative expression of the power of Reason; of man's command over nature — but not too much command; of the dignity and purposefulness of human life. It was Yeats who said, 'I have tried to make a little world out of the beautiful and pleasant and significant things of this marred and ugly world'. And here we have a little world of that kind, miraculously left us by the late eighteenth and the early nineteenth centuries. And at a slightly lower level we have here a way of escape from the values of the present day. There is no more complete form of imprisonment than to be imprisoned in the present. To allow time to destroy the

53. The Parthenon

F*

great monuments of the past is one of the most effective ways we have of cutting ourselves off from the past. If the New Town crumbled away, we could still read about Hume and Raeburn and Scott and Jeffrey and so on; we could study their work, but we wouldn't be in touch with them so well; we wouldn't understand them so well, and our understanding of the past and therefore of the present would be enfeebled.

Conservation is not a matter of being conservative, of wanting to keep things unchanged. On the contrary, it seems to me those who want to conserve are the real radicals—the constructive radicals—who are not satisfied that everything should go on as it is going. You can produce arguments of that kind about any of the fine and beautiful buildings of the past, but Edinburgh is a unique city to a large extent because of the New Town. I am sorry that some years ago Professor Rasmussen appropriated that expression 'the unique city' to apply to London. I appreciate that London has its own character but it seems to me that Edinburgh— if I may commit a solecism—is a great deal *more unique* than London! Edinburgh is a unique city, it seems to me, for three reasons. First of all, you have the visible conjuncture of the old town and the New Town. The old town is itself, of course, very fine, very interesting, but there are many other old towns, in England or in Holland or in Germany. The old town is not unique. What is unique is its co-existence with the New Town. Secondly, the New Town is unique itself, because nowhere else in the world is there a complete classical city like the New Town of Edinburgh. That is what is really so extraordinary; it is not that we have just a street or two; it is not that there is a plan that can be faintly discerned through the alterations of a century and a half. What is unique is that the whole town—buildings and streets, lanes and gardens, basements and garrets—the whole is very nearly as it was laid out, at the latest, 150 years ago. In its scale and in its completeness it has no rival, and to let the New Town go would do more to diminish the individuality of Scotland than could perhaps be done in any other way. Thirdly, there is the point that the City is not a museum—it is a living town and it is used in very much the way that it was used 100 or 150 years ago. It is threatened by two things—time and traffic: a point Colin Buchanan has already made.

One would not have to rehearse these arguments for conserving the New Town if it cost nothing, because there would be no opposition if it cost nothing—no difficulty. On the question of costs there are just two points I want to make. First, it is reasonable, it is economically reasonable, that the cost should be shared between central government, local government, and individuals. All of these parties benefit from conservation. The use of cost/benefit analysis in this matter might be helpful, not to

54. David Hume's tomb, Calton Churchyard, Edinburgh

provide some final and miraculous answer, because cost/benefit analysis doesn't do that, but in guiding one as to how the shares should be worked out between these three parties. Secondly, there is the question of the total financial cost. Sir Robert Matthew said this might be as high as £15m. One realizes that the usual way with these estimates is that they are under-estimates. Fifteen million, as he said, is a good deal of money. On the other hand, taken by itself, no figure is great and no figure is small; however large it is you can always double it; however small it is you can always half it. It's true that £15m is a lot of money if you are comparing it with the £82,000 which is the annual budget for the *Historic Buildings Council*. That, of course, may lead you to think that the £82,000 is in fact re-markably small. Rather than compare the £15m with £82,000 I think I would like to put the matter in a different light.

The replacement cost of all buildings in the personal sector in this country—that is excluding local authority houses—is about £18,550,000,000. Local authorities spend annually, on additions to the stock of housing, about £600,000,000. In the personal sector, the ex-penditure on additions to the stock of buildings is—or was a couple of years ago where one has the latest figures—about £450,000,000. So, annually, there is an expenditure on new housing in this country in excess of £1,000,000,000. Therefore, if you take this figure—this £15m figure—the rate of £750,000 per annum is three-quarters of one-tenth of one per cent of the total expenditure.

That does not seem to me too high a price to pay for the retention of a little piece of civilization.

ANDREW KERR

Conservation and the Citizen

I speak as a resident of the New Town. First, let me mention the existing situation and particularly the part played by the Corporation. It is often assumed that the Corporation is not interested in Georgian architecture: this is not the case. The Corporation is well aware of the value of Georgian Edinburgh. It has at least made a start towards conservation as envisaged by the Civic Amenities Act of 1967—that is, towards the designation of conservation areas—by the publication of two quite excellent conservation reports suggesting areas in the New Town which might be so designated. There has been criticism of the Corporation for failure, so far, actually to designate a conservation area. Many organizations and individuals have pressed, repeatedly, for immediate designation, without success. It can be argued that designation of a conservation area involves no expense, that it merely introduces special planning procedures. This is all that appears from the Act. Alternatively, it can be argued that there are financial implications in designation and that the Corporation would be forced into a positive conservation programme which would necessarily involve expense. This is, of course, the Corporation's view and it is also the view of the Scottish Development Department.

One of the purposes of the survey is to find out how much expense might be involved. I think it is clear that the whole of the New Town will eventually be designated. Between eight and nine hundred conservation areas have already been designated in Britain, and it would be absurd if the most obvious and appropriate area in the whole country were to be left out. The planning procedures which would be introduced are urgently needed and the residents are even now ready for the step to be taken. This fact in particular makes me and many other residents, for whom I speak, anxious that designation should take place as soon as possible. In the words of the Planning Department's first conservation report, to which I have already referred, 'much of the success of a conservation scheme will depend on the enthusiasm and cooperation of the public and in particular the owners and residents'.

In the last two years there has been a remarkable upsurge of interest and enthusiasm among the residents. The street associations are no longer protest groups, hastily convened in the face of a common threat, fervently signing petitions to deliver to the Lord Provost. They are constructive thinking bodies which already enjoy a mature relationship with the Corporation (which, let me say, is greatly appreciated). The associations have cooperated, particularly with the Planning Department, on many

55. View of Georgian Edinburgh

conservation matters, and are concerned with small projects of repair and replacement which are vital to conservation and which are appropriate for residents to handle. If this willingness and enthusiasm were lost, the task of conservation *eventually undertaken* would be enormously increased and the chances of substantial financial cooperation from residents—at present very good—greatly harmed.

It is suggested in the Report that the survey area should be dealt with, street by street, in cooperation with residents by means of specially formed street committees (which will not, incidentally, be necessarily related with existing street associations). A street scheme will be prepared and each street will be tackled as a whole, rather than as a string of individual buildings. You will also have been quick to observe that financial contributions by property owners are envisaged! The Bath scheme, in which property owners have contributed 25 per cent of the costs, has been quoted as an example. In all other cases to date, the owners' contribution has been greater. Now, I don't know what the owners think about this. You may feel that if everyone is making such a fuss about Georgian Edinburgh, let them get on with it (you will be glad to give the tradesmen access); or you may feel it would be appropriate to pay for a much larger percentage or even all of the necessary work. At all events, it does seem to be a reasonable argument that central government, through the *Historic Buildings Council*, should contribute in respect of the value of the New Town to the nation; the local authority should contribute in respect of the value of the New Town to the whole City of 55 Edinburgh; and property owners should contribute because their own properties are to be improved and (one imagines) increased in value.

The question which immediately occurs to residents is, of course, what if I cannot, or will not, pay my share? Time alone will show what response there will be, but in Bath, for example, there have been such cases and the work has simply not been done. In the Crescent, one house remains uncleaned among thirty-three. It will be greatly to an owner's advantage to participate in any work that is clearly necessary. All costs will be on a bulk-order basis, and consequently lower; and of course he will have to pay only a fraction of them in any case. But it is and always has been a feature of the New Town that its inhabitants vary astonishingly in means, even in the same street, and there will be owners that will not be able to afford to contribute, however small the percentage they are asked for. Total purchase is mentioned in the Conference Report, but this is scarcely very appealing to the resident who wants to stay. Even where the means exist, in the case of work which is not so clearly necessary, there will be the question of whether the street scheme represents the owner's wishes. There are many reasons for living in the New Town, of which a love of Georgian architecture is only one; and some of the work proposed may appear far from necessary to some owners. In the last six months as many astragals have been knocked out in Cumberland Street as have been replaced in Lynedoch Place. An owner is hardly likely to accept an offer to replace his astragals, however heavily subsidized, if he has just knocked them out in the name of modernization! We shall just have to hope that he will take the opportunity to have essential stone repairs carried out and so may be persuaded to join the scheme, astragals and all.

Some of the work, such as the replacement of doors and astragals, will—I hope—never have to be repeated; unless because of poor maintenance in the future. Some of the rest will last perhaps for the same period of time as it has already, say 150–200 years. Perhaps only then will it be necessary to mount a conservation operation like this again. But none of it is intended to replace, nor can it replace, the normal care of someone who lives in, knows, and loves his house. Conservation is not something that was invented for this Conference. It has been undertaken willingly by generations of residents in the past and will continue in the future. The fact that we still have the New Town to talk about at all is due to the fact that it has been looked after by our predecessors who lived in

56. No 7 Malta Terrace

it. There has been destruction and neglect, but much of what we have, including interiors, is wonderfully intact. I have mentioned the range of minor repairs and replacements undertaken by the street associations in recent years. It is these small detailed and relatively inexpensive tasks which are appropriate for residents to handle without financial assistance and I am convinced that the street associations have a real function which they are carrying out admirably.

There is much talent and expertise waiting to be tapped. Every profession is represented many times over in the New Town, and even the smallest association seems to be able to produce lawyers, architects, surveyors, accountants, and whatever else may be necessary to deal with a particular problem. There are over sixty amenity associations in Edinburgh, of which no less than forty are active in the survey area. Some of the reports and projects that have appeared in the last two years have been of the highest standard and greatest value, and much of the work could not have been carried out by outside bodies except at colossal expense. In short, it is the residents that have kept, and are still *56* keeping, the New Town alive. Without them it must necessarily die.

The New Town will not survive if those who love it, and can afford to look after it, decide to leave it. The big houses in particular, which often do not lend themselves to successful sub-division, need wealthy occupants. The New Town is an outstandingly attractive place to live in, but it could easily become less so. Its residential character must be preserved at all costs. This means keeping a careful watch on planning applications for change of use, on rateable values, and on many other factors, most important of which is adequate provision for parking — by which I mean a good chance, not half a chance, of finding somewhere to leave your car during the day. Parking and change-of-use are the two subjects that most concern residents at present. I am convinced, however, that the New Town will always be worth living in and caring for and I hope that I speak for all the residents here when I say that we welcome what this Conference proposes, wholeheartedly. We shall not be slow to play our part when the time comes and the sooner it comes, the better.

Comparative Examples

57. Grosvenor Place, Bath, after restoration

England

I think the most useful contribution I can make to this very closely-knit and well-documented Conference would be in the operational field. I can deal only with a few salient facts, past and present. I am not going to repeat anything that Sir Robert Matthew has so very ably presented already. But I must start by asking how one can place the conservation of Georgian Edinburgh in the world calendar of events, to which it undoubtedly belongs, as Count Sforza has already said. I don't believe there are any close precedents and there are certainly no exact parallels to the New Town in Edinburgh. It isn't a case of salvaging enormous monuments like the Abu Simbel Temples on the Nile; it is not even, really, a case of preserving a fabulous concentration of works of art and architecture from the mud and the water, as in Venice. Nevertheless, I think if the total decay of classical Edinburgh occurred it would be a loss to world culture. It would have the dimensions of what the press nowadays calls a disaster, and I believe the remedy for this has got to be commensurate with the possibility of the damage.

The slow accident of time has brought the New Town of Edinburgh to the same building situation as earthquake did in Lisbon and as fire did in the City of London.

It is interesting that, just precisely one hundred years before Craig was working on his plan, came Wren's plan for the rebuilding of the city of London in 1666. Craig's plan was accurately described by Professor Youngson just two hundred years later—that is, in 1966—as entirely sensible and almost painfully orthodox, but the point is that it was *well* built—that it *was* built and it was *well* built—with fine and sometimes loving detail; and it posed no impossible standards of grandeur or of cost to prevent its extensions being carried on for another hundred years, to make a most wonderfully greater whole. Now Wren's plan was quite different. It was an architectural and intellectual *tour de force*. But what was actually built under the improved regulations and the rough but practical justice of the Fire Courts of those days (where you and I, if we owned property, would go and make our case) was a much more homespun thing. Wren's genius flowered instead in St Paul's and the City churches, and elsewhere. So, in spite of royal patronage and the special concern of Parliament (which put a special tax on coal and corn delivered into London, in order to finance the rebuilding of the City) the main burden of restoration was actually spread over the owners and occupiers, in Guilds, in parishes, in businesses, down to the smallest.

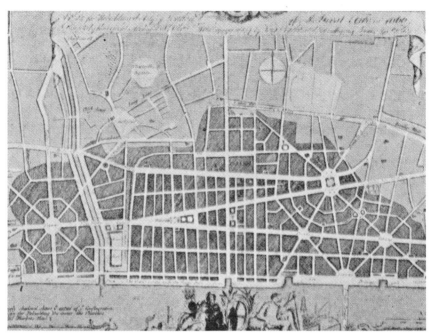

58. Wren's Plan for London, 1666

In other words, the operation was an emergency one, financed jointly by public and private resources.

Three hundred years later, in our pursuit of liberty, equality, and utility, we have in fact required the raising of taxation in many forms: income tax, death duties, capital gains tax, selective employment tax, and even motor taxes—to such an extent that no private landlord can maintain a really big estate, no private fortune can endow it, as the *National Trust* is beginning now to find. Householders, even in co-operation, cannot afford restoration costs of the kind required in the New Town. So once again the Exchequer has to prime the pump before a major salvage operation can get under way. Many of the masons, of course, have moved to better-paid employment and it is quite a job to bring them back, but they can be brought back. Building costs are rising—more than five per cent a year—and maintenance and restoration costs by nearly ten per cent a year. This is a fact which is not generally recognized, but it is crucial to the work of the *Historic Buildings Council*, and is crucial to the conservation of Georgian Edinburgh.

The Government has raised from £570,000 to £700,000 the amount of grants which the *Historic Buildings Council for England* could recommend in the current financial year. This is the generosity towards which the

Lord Provost referred and I cannot imagine that the rise in the Scottish rate would be any less. So, you see, the pump-priming process is accelerating. Sir Robert Matthew mentioned that the grants of the *Historic Buildings Council for Scotland* were £82,000, and we have heard from Lord Hughes that the allowance over the next three years will be roughly (I suppose) about £110,000. But the important point that I am trying to make is that in a thing of disaster dimensions like this the contribution to the New Town will have to be outwith this ration.

I have been concerned with the listing and preservation of historic buildings in England since the wartime planning act of 1944, and a member of the *Historic Buildings Council for England* since its creation in 1953. At that time Parliament had voted £250,000 a year to cover our grant recommendations. In 1955 the figure went up to £350,000, and we wrote in our 1954 report—that was, in our *second* report—that the problem of whole terraces of houses would have to be given special attention. It arose in a most acute form in Bath, where the number and importance of the terraces, and I am quoting from the report,

> made it a national as well as a local problem. It is clear that to deal with individual applications from owners would be undesirable, as the piecemeal restoration of the facade of a terrace was likely to be much more expensive in total than a comprehensive programme of repair and might produce an unfortunate lack of uniformity.

We visited Bath, therefore, to meet representatives of the City Corporation and the *Preservation Trust* and agreed with them that a joint committee of the three organizations, together with independent members, should be set up to submit to the *Historic Buildings Council* and to Bath Corporation detailed proposals for the restoration of outstanding terraces in Bath. In addition to the amount which the owners themselves could contribute, grants would be offered under the Historic Buildings legislation and supplemented by grants from the Corporation. We hoped— and I am sorry to lower the temperature a little here—that expenditure at the rate of about £10,000 per annum might be achieved and although the immediate effects might not be great, we hoped that in ten years' time this procedure would produce a notable result in Bath. Well, in spite of the smallness of that sum, it has; and those of you who have recently *59-61* seen the *Circus*, for example, will recognize what has been done.

This led to the initiation of what the Council call *Town Schemes*. There are now twenty in England, and more in the pipeline, but the grants are still small. The *Historic Buildings Council's* contribution is normally 25 per cent—not 50 per cent as is now obviously proposed here. The local authorities produce 25 per cent, and sometimes that is divided between the County and the Borough or District Council. The owners produce the

59. The Circus, Bath, before restoration

other 50 per cent or half the total. The vote from Parliament has to cover
not just the Town Schemes, and great mansions like Blenheim or Castle
Howard, but also over 300,000 listed buildings, large and small, which
may become—will become, probably—eligible for grants. So I think
it is worth looking for a brief moment at other operations of a special
character.

The first is Regent's Park—also terraces. In 1957, the Crown estate faced
the future of the Nash terraces in Regent's Park—here we are talking of
only 374 complete houses, as against something like 3,500 properties,
as they are called, in the New Town survey. But it is still a formidable
operation, and they had already spent £2·5m on them in repairing war
damage. The Gorrel Committee in 1946 had said they were of national
importance and that 'they should be preserved as far as that is practicable'
(ominous word) 'and without strict regard to the economics of prudent
estate management'. But the commissioners, who had the great advantage
of being a single landlord in this case, preferred comprehensive redevelopment, considerable conversion of the houses into flats—sometimes horizontally—and of course much higher rents. The big problem,
they said, was the structural condition. We would not recommend very
large amounts of capital being expended unless they would result in a
further life for the buildings of at least sixty years. But, the risks taken by
the Crown Estate at Regent's Park have, in the event, been economically
justified. They were not only prudent but also profitable and, in Colin
Buchanan's words, they counted the cost and they are now starting to
reap considerable benefit.

My second example is Oxford. The problem, here, is very much a
matter of masonry. In Edinburgh, roughly 67 per cent of the total cost is
likely to be masonry. In Oxford, it was over 85 per cent. But, in 1959,
the University and Colleges launched a public appeal for the repair of
their historic buildings—mostly in stone—on which they had spent
£300,000 in the previous 10 years—and they concluded that the task
of major restoration was too great for them to finance without impairing
their vital academic responsibilities. Now the sum required was
£2,090,000, to be spread over 10 years. £340,000 of it came from their
own resources, and £1·75m was raised by appeal. The late Lord Bridges,
you may remember, was a prime mover in this. Now it is worth noting
that the *Historic Buildings Council for England* was allowed by the Minister
to contribute £15,000 a year under an approved scheme, item by item.
That is to say we visited the buildings, saw what was proposed to be
done to them and approved it, as it were—before the money was paid out.
This was, of course, just one twenty-fifth of the sum which is going to be

60. The Circus, Bath during restoration

61. Pulteney Street, Bath, after restoration

expected, from the *Scottish Historic Buildings Council,* for Edinburgh.

The third example is an even smaller one—it is Eton. Eton College School—and you might almost call it a small town—had to face a capital expenditure at the end of the war of about £3m, which was spread over the following twenty to twenty-five years. The founder, Henry VI, had made provision—this was in the fifteenth century—for a current expenditure account, and also a capital fund, so that the foundation could share with the King's scholars the benefits of a very far-sighted endowment. A war damage payment of £98,000 did no more than 'establish the *status quo*', as Mr McConnel says in his recent book, *Eton Repointed*. There was thus a massive programme of delayed maintenance (they did no maintenance during the whole of the nineteenth century), restoration, re-equipment, and new building. In the end—this is the interesting point—the foundation, that is, Henry VI's foundation, supplied one third of the necessary capital sums; the Farrow Bequests and other Trusts provided the second third; and the Eton appeal raised the final third from 5,000 individual donors. This large and ancient comprehensive school near Slough—as it has been satirically but also very accurately described—is now better equipped in physical terms than it has ever been, and a fairly major operation of preservation and change has been carried out entirely without recourse to public funds. There are many other examples besides these three—I have quoted these three because I know them and because they offer some points of comparison with the much larger problem facing Edinburgh.

The target of £15m suggested as a result of the Edinburgh Architectural Association's survey seems to me to be reasonable, but I think it would clearly be better spent over 15 years than 20, if the will is there and the organization is effective. The momentum is kept up by having in fact a shorter period. One realizes, of course, the difficulty of getting contractors, masons, and all the other people organized for this. The examples I have given you, however, show that people have been able to take extraordinary steps to build more quickly, now, than one has been used to in the last fifty years. In St Andrews, when golfing hours are reduced in the winter, they keep themselves warm by litigation. If this can be avoided in Edinburgh, there is no knowing what splendid results could be achieved! When you come down to it, finance and administration are the big problems and the big challenges. The administration, if it runs smoothly, can save an enormous amount of time. It is not for anyone born south, not only of the border but also of the equator, to suggest what proportion of the capital required might be raised directly from Government or, through local government, by the local authority; how much from Trusts, Foundations, and Bequests; how much by public

62/63. Sedan chair houses at rear of Queen Square, Bath, before and after restoration

appeal; how much from owners and occupiers; how much from secured loans. There are, however, two things an outside observer can say: first, that the objective is worthwhile nationally, internationally, and locally, not only in a public but also in a private domestic residential sense; and, secondly, that the funds and resources should, I think like a pyramid, have as wide a popular base as possible and as great a height as the government in power can be persuaded to build them! I hope I have made my single point—that this is a complex form of combined operations and I wish it every possible success.

LE MARAIS

LE TEMPLE

PLAN TURGOT

FRANÇOIS SORLIN

Paris

To the best of my knowledge—and it has already been said by others—the *New Town* of Edinburgh has no equivalent in the world. The problem is not therefore to determine if it will be preserved : it *has* to be preserved. It is how it is to be saved from the pressures of modern life and from decay that concerns us. This is, of course, a unique problem for you to solve. Nevertheless, it may be useful for you to know the way in which other countries—such as France—try to solve similarly difficult problems. Let us take, for instance, the case of the *Marais* district in Paris. This part of Paris is one of forty *secteurs sauvegardés*—that is, Conservation Areas—which were created in France in 1962 by means of the Act of 4th August of that year, which is generally known as *la loi Malraux*—André Malraux, as Minister of Culture, was the principal progenitor of the law. Among those *secteurs sauvegardés*, the Marais is the most important, not only because it is the largest, but because it is one of the districts of the capital, and sustains one of the most valuable messages we inherit from our history.

The Marais has been inhabited since the beginning of the eleventh century though the buildings of that time were demolished during the Middle Ages. It was so called because it occupied the site of an ancient marsh on the left bank of the Seine. After the demolition of the first Marais during the fourteenth and fifteenth centuries, a new area was created at the beginning of the sixteenth.

We can see this area on the famous Plan Turgot. That Plan shows Paris in 1739, including the quarter with the famous *Place Royale*, created by the order of King Henry IV. Around it many aristocratic houses were built at the end of the sixteenth and at the beginning of the seventeenth century. During the seventeenth and eighteenth centuries these mansions were gradually abandoned by their inhabitants, as there was created, on the other bank of the Seine, a new area, called *le Faubourg Saint Germain*. Fashion drew the inhabitants of the Marais towards the Faubourg Saint Germain, and then the Marais began to be inhabited not by the nobility, but by workmen, who pervaded the district and began to transform the mansions into workshops or warehouses. The majestic rooms of those mansions were then partitioned to form living accommodation or workshops. The district remained in a very poor condition until the French Government, very recently, decided to undertake its revival, by means of the 1962 Act.

The rehabilitation of this area presents a very long and hard task.

64

65

66

64. (*facing*) The Plan Turgot, a graphic representation of the Marais in 1763
65. (*overleaf*) A plan of the Marais today, showing how courtyards and gardens have been built up
66. (*overleaf*) A plan of the Marais as it will be when restoration is complete

LE MARAIS

ETAT ACTUEL

LE MARAIS

ETAT FUTUR

67. L'hôtel de Sully, before restoration (1920)

67, 68 The French Ministry of Cultural Affairs and the City Council of Paris have, however, already bought some of the finest *hôtels*, in order to restore them to their former state, such as the *Hôtel de Béthune Sully* in the Rue St Antoine, which belonged to Sully, the Minister of Henry IV. During the nineteenth century a central part was added, and the building progressively lost its original appearance, becoming a kind of workshop with boutiques; the arcades were completely hidden at the *rez-de-chaussée*. After we had bought this hôtel, in 1962, we began the first stages of restoration. The central part was demolished and the original proportions re-established. The interior, as well as the exterior, was then completely restored. Now the *hôtel* is the seat of the *Caisse Nationale des Monuments Historiques de France*. This kind of operation, however, is not what we should call a revitalization of areas of historic interest. It is a *normal* operation of restoring an ancient building. It should not be considered as the beginning of the Marais operation, which is to be envisaged not as a series of separate enterprises, but as a whole.

The Marais is still cluttered with buildings erected during the eighteenth and nineteenth centuries, especially by artisans. Almost all the courtyards, where before there were ancient gardens and courtyards, are now hidden by garages and by workshops. Our ambition is to re-establish the former

68. L'hôtel de Sully, after restoration in 1970

state. We want to recreate the gardens, to demolish the workshops,
and to restore the exteriors and interiors of buildings. It is a very difficult
task; according to statistics, sixty per cent of the dwellings in the Marais
have no toilet, thirty per cent no running water, fifteen per cent no
electricity. A conservation and enhancement plan has been prepared by
a team of architects and town planners for a total area of about 450 acres,
that is, about 200 hectares. This plan allows for the demolition of all the
accretions and for the re-establishment of the condition prevailing in   *69, 70*
the Turgot Plan. These operations are not technically complex, but the
costs of so ambitious an undertaking are high, and tend to increase, and
therefore create a serious financial problem.

One of the first operations begun since the 1962 Law was the restoration of the *Hôtel Guénégaud*. It is an operation, not of restoration, but
of revitalization of an ancient mansion. The hôtel was previously in a
very bad state. A wall had been built between the two wings, and the
original garden had disappeared. That wall was demolished and the hotel
was restored. A two-storeyed underground car park was created beneath
the courtyard, the entrance to which is invisible from the street. Afterwards, the gardens, which can be seen on the Turgot Plan, were relaid.

We come now to the problem of new uses of restored hôtels or buildings.

69. Painted ceilings uncovered during restoration of l'hôtel de Savourny in 1970

70. The same ceilings restored

(In France a hôtel is a mansion.) It is a very delicate one, since the size and the shape of the reception rooms is no longer relevant to the needs of modern living. The only solution for the revitalization of the 300 large residences in the Marais is to use them for embassies or head offices of large companies. In the case of the *Hôtel Guénégaud*, the chosen solution was that of a museum. But one can hardly imagine 300 museums in the Marais. However, the area does not solely comprise large *hôtels* like the *Guénégaud* but also more than 1,500 dwelling houses—plain houses of historic or artistic interest, with numerous carvings, ironworks, or paintings.

The work of restoration of these houses is going to be undertaken in what we call a *secteur expérimental*—that is, experimental area in the heart of the *secteur sauvegardé*. Here are some of the large residences to which I have referred, the *Hôtel Lamoignon*, the *Hôtel Carnavalet* which is a museum of the City Council, and the *Hôtel Salé*, which has one of the most impressive staircases of Paris. Between those mansions are many smaller houses, which are still habitable, and in which very poor people live. We cannot expel them from the Marais, because if we did so we would go against not only the letter but the spirit of our law of revitalization. This is one of our main principles: the revitalization—*the rehabilitation*—of our old quarters cannot be made regardless of the wishes of the inhabitants; we cannot act *against* that population. It is necessary to obtain a real understanding between those who live in the houses, and the authorities in charge of the restoration. There are more than 250 main houses, and we want the population of artisans to go on living there, providing them with the same means of work and same means of living as they had before the restoration began. If we did not do so, all the population would turn against the authorities—against both the local and the national authorities—inside the whole area. That is the reason why the social aspect of the revitalization is so important. We have to work with the population; not against it.

The experimental area contains at least ten very interesting mansions. The *Hôtel de Marle*, while not one of the most important, is still one of   *71, 72* the more significant in the experimental area. It has been bought by the Swedish Government, and I think there may be some cultural legacy brought to it from that country on account of its use. At present we are demolishing the workshops which were in the courtyard, and at the same time are building beneath the courtyard and gardens (now re-designed) underground car-parks. After demolishing the accretions, brought into the house by workmen during the past centuries, the old timber frame was found to be intact. Some of the houses in this area were

71. L'hôtel de Marle, hidden by parasite buildings in 1968

in very poor condition, as well as being encumbered by new work. Once these accretions have been removed the beautiful old architecture appears again. We modernize the flats inside at the same time as restoring the outside. We have discovered painted ceilings in nearly every house in the experimental area. These we restore to their primary state, as they were at the beginning of the seventeenth century.

The restoration of the *Hôtel de St Aignan* required another kind of work, the demolition of upper storeys added in the nineteenth century. The house belongs to the City Council, who have given the use of it to the *International Council of Monuments and Sites*. Much work remains **73, 74** to be done before it can be occupied. The *Hôtel Liberal Bruant* is one of the most famous mansions in the Marais. The architect, Liberal Bruant — one of the greatest of the seventeenth century — built Les Invalides. This was his house. It was abandoned and half-hidden by a garage.

Another kind of operation now proceeding is the creation of new architecture inside the historic fabric of the Marais. This is a very difficult problem, which has not yet been solved in a very satisfactory way in France (as indeed in other countries). A project, proposed by the Ministere de Postes for a new Central Telephone Exchange in the centre of the Marais was out of scale with the historic fabric, so we refused it.

72. L'hôtel de Marle, restored in 1970

73. L'hôtel Liberal Bruant, before restoration

74. L'hôtel Liberal Bruant, during restoration in 1970

Another kind of problem is that of commerce. Very often the arcades at the *rez-de-chaussée* were hidden by boutiques built during the eighteenth and nineteenth centuries. One of our aims is to remove the boutiques and recreate the arcades. On the Plan Turgot may be seen *Place Royale* (now renamed Place des Vosges). Under the arcades we have created new shops, which are fully incorporated into the architecture of the arcade. It is a very long and difficult process, but we are now beginning to succeed in obtaining, from all the people who live here, permission to destroy the boutiques and to recreate the old arcades.

Let us now come to the important and related problem of traffic and parking, which forms one of the principal instruments of potential destruction in historic towns, as Professor Buchanan reminded us. The cracking of frail structures within ancient buildings by the repeated vibration of vehicles, especially by heavy vehicles; the increasing erosion of stone through the emission of harmful fumes: these are some of the main problems which are now before us, and which we must solve if we want to revitalize our old towns. In the case of the Marais, the greatest possible effort was made, as you can see from photographs showing the underground car parks now in construction, to conserve and enhance the plan and fabric of the town by creating relief roads round the historic core. But the Marais is located in the heart of a capital city, making it difficult to create more peripheral highways in the town network. That is why as many underground car parks as possible are included in the restoration works.

And now comes the main question which has been posed many times — what does it cost? I must not hide the fact that those operations are expensive. Expense cannot be avoided at the beginning of an experiment like this, but as the job went on we got a rather agreeable surprise. The works which we were afraid were going to be very costly turned out to be not so expensive as we had thought when we looked at the problem of re-establishing the conditions prevailing at the time of the Turgot Plan. Now, after six years of experiment, we can say that the cost is lower than we feared. As you know, our rental system, about which I cannot explain in detail here, is based on the use of mixed-society economics, which work for the good of the *local* authorities, *national* authorities, and the *landlords* together. Those societies pay about eighty per cent of the total expenditure, twenty per cent of which comes from subsidies and sixty per cent from grants or loans from the State or from the City. During the first five years, the subsidies and the loans have been given by the State and by the City Council without any counterpart from land-lords. But at this stage a monetary contribution comes in from the landlords *after* the completion of the works; that money is very useful indeed for carrying out further restoration. As it is, we are now rich enough to begin a new experiment in the Marais. I must add that the car parks are bought as soon as they are completed so that other underground car parks can be built continuously. This kind of operation is naturally expensive but—and this is very important—not more so than the cost of demolishing and rebuilding new houses, even if we include the cost of the gardens and courtyards. So I must say that, considering the difficulties encountered, the results are rather encouraging; but—and this is the main point with which I want to conclude—the success of such an experiment leads public opinion to take a growing interest in the cultural heritage of our old towns. I am quite sure that here in Edinburgh, where you have such a precious cultural heritage, you will find the appropriate means to restore and enhance your beautiful New Town. I give all my best wishes for your courageous and doubtlessly successful enterprise.

75. L'hôtel de Braque

Summing-up and Discussion

PATRICK NUTTGENS

The Principles of Conservation

In the last few years, there have been a number of absolutely fundamental studies done in England on various towns, in relation to their conservation. But the scale of the proposed operation in Edinburgh makes the work at York, or Bath, or Chichester, or Chester relatively small and trivial. The area of the Georgian New Town of Edinburgh is something like three times the entire city of mediaeval York and considerably more than that of the present conservation area; ten times the Bath conservation area, and something like four times, I suppose, the size of Georgian Bath; and about ten times that of the Chester conservation. So the scale is really an unprecedented one even to talk about. I shall try to isolate a number of the issues in any conservation pattern that seem to me to throw some light on the problems that are contained in this situation. I have no doubt that, as in most academic pursuits, the obscurity deepens as the clarifications proceed.

There seem to me to be seven items which might be useful in such a discussion; and three big conclusions at the end. First of all, I think that every one of these studies in conservation, and the discussions we have had today, emphasize that we are concerned with the totality of a place, and not with its individual items. As far as conservation is concerned, buildings and landscape are one; an attitude of mind that represents a change of policy from what we used to think about even a few years ago. It is particularly appropriate to say this in relation to the New Town, because the New Town, in its foundation and its extensions, was a plan and an idea for a total community of all classes and all kinds of functions and trades. Its squares and streets and lanes and yards were in fact a way of providing a total kind of community development. Conservationists are accused of being a middle-class movement. This is to a large extent true, but the areas which conservationists are concerned to conserve are total areas and not merely one-class areas. That seems to me a crucial principle of anything to do with conservation. To put it in a more imaginative way—painting up the Town hall in the middle of the twilight area is not conservation; leaving the Town Hall to fall down while doing up the surrounding area *is* conservation.

The second point is this: any conservation policy seems to me to require the knowledge of what category one is dealing with, including its size and its future. Conservation implies the completion of an area, not the further subdivision of it. Conservation is largely the completion of potential patterns. Thirdly, conservation always involves a degree

76. St Vincent Street, Edinburgh

77. Traffic in Princes Street, Edinburgh

of elimination, the removal of the accretions and the unnecessary, as M. Sorlin has shown us. Discovering the underlying unity and the underlying structure of a place is really no different from the conservation of a building. It consists largely of the removal of the unnecessary and the discovery of the reality which was lurking in the background all the time. Fourthly, conservation always seems to imply something to do with tourism. As we enter a new phase of our national life, any conservation exercise must take into consideration the element of the outside person's interest in the area. There are different scales of appreciation of a place for those living in it, living near it, and visiting it from time to time.

Fifthly, any conservation exercise, as Professor Buchanan has pointed out, involves a consideration of traffic. This has possibly more to do with traffic management than with total traffic planning and traffic reorganization. That seems to me an important concept about a place, and it often involves a reversal of ground on figure and figure on ground (rather as modern painting does) of what you see as the main components and the minor ones. Looking a little while ago at a large northern city, I found myself baffled to think what had been the image in the mind of the person designing the modern road system until it occurred to me— and I speak with great respect—that he was a brilliant designer of

77

sewage systems! If you interpret that road system as an enormous sewage system in which cars are bits of sewage going along and gradually merging and flowing without interruption until they land in the sea, it is impeccable. It may be we want a kind of inverted, back-running, sewage system which operates in conservation.

The sixth thing is—and I don't think this has been mentioned much today—that any conservation policy must involve—even when the element of preservation is enormous—a code of *design*. Conservation does not mean standing still: it is in fact an act of designing, changing, completing, and altering. Some kind of code of design is necessary for the details shown by Sir Robert, and for the total groups of buildings shown by M. Sorlin. Some code, some principle of design as to what is appropriate is absolutely essential. That in itself involves describing clearly in words what the place is and what it is about.

The seventh point is that any conservation exercise involves *housing*. It is essentially a housing exercise because nearly all conservation involves buildings which were houses which are in process of change; and therefore it must, as a social exercise, be tied to consideration of housing. Housing in this country appears to be at least entering a new phase, in which rehabilitation may be more important than the total demolition and redevelopment of old places for new ones. As Count Sforza was indicating, the younger generations are interested in old property brought up to date, so the whole conservation process and policy must be tied to a housing policy for all groups, and at all kinds of costs. The Housing Acts, and the very much increased grants available for improvement, must be relevant to the situation.

Three conclusions seem to me to come out of all our exercises. The first one is that conservation is really no different from town planning. It has the same philosophy, the same approach. What Sir Patrick Geddes was doing in the Lawnmarket in the way of survey and analysis and plan is no different from what a good conservation planner should be doing today. It is very difficult to see what are the real costs of conservation as opposed to what you ought to be doing anyway: conservation is the same as planning, only a good deal more so. Secondly, conservation is clearly an exercise in participation. Most of it arises from the alarm that we all feel about what is happening to environments that we know; and it derives from our preference (which gets clearer and clearer every year and is now unmistakeable) for what we already have, particularly when it happens to be extraordinarily good. The enormous increase in the civic society movement, the consumer movement (things of that kind), are all part of the pattern. And the fact that the Edinburgh architects were able to do this work voluntarily is itself symptomatic of this participatory exercise; as is the fact that we are all here today. The third and last conclusion is that it seems to me inevitable that conservation must involve the partnership of local initiative and central help. The local authority studying, producing the policies and the initiative; the civic societies putting on pressure in involving money; the owners and central government producing grants where they are necessary. That partnership involves little things, and little bits of work and change, as well as major works: it may even be that the smaller efforts are just as important, or more important, than the big ones.

Processes take a very long time to get off the ground, but when they do, something really can happen. If the grants made available to Edinburgh's improvement of the New Town were the same as those that were used for Bath, it would take 800 years to complete the work; and even the Government, with its well-known ability to compromise and postpone, has not yet produced a planning policy based on that time scale.

Ultimately, we are involved with costs and with money. It is a remarkable achievement that the architects and surveyors and others of this City should have spent so much time in entirely free work to produce this study and this Report.

78. Mylne's Court, Lawnmarket, Edinburgh, after restoration

Discussion

During a vigorous general discussion, based on a selection of written questions, with supplementaries from the floor, and with replies from the platform, the audience made known its concern on a wide range of issues. Although these hinged on the role of, and threat to, the New Town, some did not directly relate to the conservation of its fabric, which was the subject of the Conference. The Chairman explained that the platform could not therefore become involved in such discussion, yet he was aware of the relevance of these wider aspects to the specific problem, and a certain amount of airing of views would no doubt help to clarify the attitudes of the authorities concerned in these matters. Specifically, it was not envisaged that the Committee which it was proposed to set up should in any way concern itself with, or attempt to abrogate, the proper functions of the town planning bodies. 'The machinery we are suggesting is an *aid* to the Corporation in its wider town planning power.'

Priorities. There was a minority view that the conference had got its values and priorities wrong. Edinburgh had no modern sewage purification plant, and every day millions of gallons of untreated sewage were pumped into the Firth of Forth. 'Can one honestly preserve buildings and yet live in a sea of filth?' Again, 20,000 houses in Edinburgh were without baths. Did the conference consider the restoration of astragals in the New Town more urgent than these questions of pollution and health? 'Surely baths are more important in anybody's estimation?' The Chairman replied that such views were not relevant to the function of the conference. Society was always faced with a wide variety of desirable objectives, but these were not strictly alternatives, and it should be recognized that the deliberate abandonment of one set of objectives was not likely, in political terms, to achieve the attainment of another set. A deliberate decision to allow the New Town to decay, and thus to save £15m over 20 years, was unlikely to increase the supply of baths.

Function. A more relevant issue, touched on by several speakers, concerned function. The term 'New Town', taken in conjunction with the statement that it was 'remarkably intact' suggested that it continued to perform its original role. This was hardly so. First, it had been built as a northern suburb of the old town and had now become the city centre. Second, it had been built as a residential area, and was rapidly becoming a shopping centre and office accommodation. Third, it had been built as an integrated social unit, and what residential housing remained had been priced beyond the reach of all but a small percentage of the population of Edinburgh. 'Is there a risk of a restored New Town becoming an enclave of a certain class of people and not a mix of population?' Similar problems had been noted by M. Sorlin in connection with the *Marais*, and only tentative solutions had been suggested. What *kind* of New Town was the conference trying to conserve? In so far as members of the platform felt called on to reply to questions of this nature, their answers were that a function of conservation was precisely to call a halt to the process of erosion of the New Town as a residential area for a wide social mix; and in fact, in the narrower thoroughfares of Craig's *New Town*, and in its northern extensions, such as Cumberland Street for instance, small flats and houses, with modest rateable values, still abounded. 'The shape and composition of the New Town area as we have defined it will ensure that there is a very large range of incomes going to be housed within that area, and I hope that the policies will be directed to that end.'

Traffic. The third major issue concerned transportation policy. It was argued that this could not be excluded from the discussion on the grounds that it did not concern the *fabric*. The principal speakers had all stressed that pollution and vibration caused by traffic could be a major factor in the decay of the stonework. Colin Buchanan had specifically said that the traffic problem was 'directly relevant to the preservation of the fabric' and 'directly relevant to the subject of the conference'. Again, speakers had recognized that the primary, residential role of the New Town was rapidly becoming incompatible with the use of its principal streets as major traffic arteries. The city's plan to divert traffic from the heart of the New Town by means of an inner-ring road, which seemed to many like putting it in a hangman's noose, had been vigorously and successfully contested at government level by those very amenity societies, street associations, and private residents who had been invited to the conference to support its aims. The substitute of an eastern link road seemed to many of these little more than a subterfuge—'a sneaky underhand way'—for the original scheme. They regarded this issue as central to the whole problem of conservation, and expected their views to be taken note of. The platform accepted the vigorous expression of these views but regretted that they did not come within the terms of reference of the conference, and consequently could not be given official responses. Professor Buchanan, however, said that any answer to the traffic problem was bound to involve some compromise, 'bound to involve taking property somewhere': the smallest measure of compromise compatible with the objective of conserving the New Town as a place for living in. A 'base load of traffic' in the area had to be accepted and planned for if the central area of the city was to remain, 'a powerful, viable, commercial centre'. In assessing priorities, in attempting a cost/benefit 'of the aesthetic satisfaction of conservation to generations of inhabitants and visitors', take this audience attending the conference, giving up time to attend, travelling far and wide to attend. Such an audience, said Mr Buchanan, was bound to add up to 'a very considerable sum of money' on the side of conservation. The Chairman commented: 'Here we are—one enormous cost benefit. *Look at us*!'

Immediacy. Many members of the audience were concerned that, in delegating to any new Committee the responsibility of urging on the national and civic authorities a large-scale plan for conservation, which was bound to be long-term, the energies of the many smaller organizations individually concerned with aspects of conservation might be dissipated, and inertia replace useful activity. In the interim, before the big scheme got up steam, the process of erosion might continue, even gather speed. The case of the demolition of the *Scottish Life Association* building, in Princes Street, was relevant. Scottish lawyers, willy-nilly, were at the heart of the matter, for 'so long as they continued to interpret the laws of conservation and of payment of compensation as they had hitherto', the Corporation 'could not risk paying the compensation necessary' and demolition would therefore continue. St James' Square was 'totally obliterated'. There were great new holes in St Andrew Square. Would the Civic Trust not step in and 'lend financial support to the next preservation issue where there was unanimity of opinion that a preservation order should be made on a building'? Unless this were done, several speakers doubted whether Section v of the Civic Amenities Act, requiring *positive* planning permission to pull down a statutorily listed building, might still lack teeth.

Mr Duncan Sandys had said 'to tackle the task piecemeal would produce unsatisfactory results'. This was accepted, but unfortunately deterioration operates piecemeal, and a certain amount of piecemeal work was therefore justified. The amenity societies, the street associations, and individual owners should all be encouraged to go on with pilot schemes and individual enterprises. 'Pilot schemes of restoration should be encouraged, assisted by the fullest use of existing arrangements. Melville Street obviously comes to mind.' For instance, when City Engineer's notices were served on owners of a listed building, to remedy defects, could stronger action not in future be taken to ensure that such repairs were properly and fittingly carried out to a high standard? 'Where basic structural stone' was involved, it should be made certain that the work was satisfactorily completed before withdrawing the notice. 'Where decorative stone' was involved, the repairs 'should be grant-earning'. 'In this way, we can get down to current needs. These notices come a few at a time and we can grasp a manageable problem and learn how to tackle the whole'. The experience of all these smaller scale enterprises would be valuable and accumulative.

In this connection Count Sforza noted the twofold value of a European conservation organization. The question of decaying stone was common to Venice and Versailles, to Amsterdam and Edinburgh. The causes might well be similar and if so, remedies applied in one case might be relevant to all. Such a pool of information would be most valuable. Second, protest against desecration of the architectural heritage, if organized on a European scale, would—did—have far more effect upon the governments finally responsible than merely national or local protest.

Among other points raised was the possibility of establishing a fund to which the public could subscribe, with the object of assisting in the conservation plan. Such a fund would be additional to the moneys contributed by Government, local authority, and owners. This was welcomed. The Chairman also agreed to put to the conference an addition to the main resolution, noting the continuing importance of the role of the amenity and local associations.

The Recommendations

Resolution at the conclusion of the Conference on the Conservation of Georgian Edinburgh organized by the Scottish Civic Trust in collaboration with the Civic Trust, London, and the Edinburgh Architectural Association and held in the Assembly Rooms, Edinburgh, on 6 June 1970.

That this Conference welcomes the Report on the conservation of Georgian Edinburgh submitted by the Conference Committee under the Chairmanship of Sir Robert Matthew, warmly congratulates the authors, re-emphasizes the unique importance of Georgian Edinburgh to our national and architectural heritage, and calls upon the Scottish Civic Trust to start forthwith negotiations for the setting-up of an advisory committee as recommended in the Report so that the necessary steps can be taken with the practical and financial support of central government and the local authority to achieve the conservation of Georgian Edinburgh along the lines indicated in the Report and in the light of the views expressed during this conference.

To meet the valuable point raised in the discussion by Mr Colin McWilliam, the following was added to the Resolution:

The conference further calls upon all bodies concerned in the meantime and until such new arrangements can be made, to use to the maximum the powers and grants already available for the conservation of the New Town.

The Resolution was then put to the conference. It was carried by a very large majority, three voting against it.

Appendix: The Conference Booklet

INTRODUCTION

Why 'New Town'? The writer of Ecclesiastes who claimed that 'there is no new thing under the sun' might have cause to recant when faced with some of our technological advances, but not over the concept of the New Town, for it was introduced into Edinburgh in 1767 for much the same reasons which have led to the growth of its modern counterparts.

The New Town of Edinburgh, like them, was the joint project of many interests, private, civic, and national: but the outcome of the efforts of these concerted interests was a unique example of Georgian town planning and distinguished architecture which has gained international fame over the years.

Although it is the case that Edinburgh's New Town has remained remarkably intact, its external condition is now depreciating rapidly, and it is subject to heavy pressures of various kinds. Even before the passing of the Civic Amenities Act in 1967, and through it the creation of the Conservation Area concept, it had become clear that a cooperation of interests similar to that which originally produced the New Town would be needed today if its fabric is to be conserved and its vitality maintained, while it serves the modern needs of those who use it.

How The Rescue Operation Was Mounted. When the Scottish Civic Trust was founded in May 1967, one of its Trustees, Sir Robert Matthew, urged that the Trustees should make the fabric of the New Town of Edinburgh one of its most urgent concerns. The moment seemed ripe. The Melville Street and Melville Crescent pilot project instituted by the Historic Buildings Council for Scotland and Edinburgh Corporation had been launched as the first preservation project in the joint operation by the HBC and Edinburgh Corporation. During the 1968 Festival the exhibition 'Two Hundred Summers in a City' greatly aroused public interest in the history and architectural merit of the New Town.

Accordingly, the Trustees as soon as possible sought the collaboration of the Edinburgh Architectural Association, which first under the Presidency of Mr James Dunbar-Nasmith and then under that of Mr B. V. K. Cottier, mustered a team of over one hundred and twenty architects, surveyors, engineers, and others, who volunteered to give generously of their time and skills to carry out an external fabric survey of every property in a pre-designated area of over two hundred streets, comprising the concentrated centre of Edinburgh's Georgian development.

It should be emphasized that, while Conservation as a whole involves other major questions, this Survey and Conference are concentrated exclusively on the condition of the fabric of the New Town, and the remedial measures necessary.

Unfortunately, it was not possible to include every worthwhile Georgian development in Edinburgh within the scope of the present survey. The exclusion of such areas, streets or houses outside the main Georgian centre, does not imply that they are not equally worthy of conservation. Indeed, one of the differences between the situation which confronts Bath and that which confronts Edinburgh is that whereas Georgian Bath represents the most extensive aspect of that city's whole conservation problem, Georgian development, of which the New Town forms by far the major sector, is only part of Edinburgh's architectural heritage.

Some of the findings of the Edinburgh Architectural Association's Report are dealt with in a later section of these Conference Papers.

Beyond Words Into Action. The Edinburgh Architectural Association's Report will be published, together with the proceedings and conclusions of this Conference and a generous photographic supplement included, it is hoped, as quickly as possible. The purpose of this publication will be to provide a guide to aid practical conservation over a period of possibly twenty years. Undoubtedly, a conservation exercise on this scale launched with so much voluntary effort will also be of interest and example to Governments, Local Authorities, Universities and Planning Schools throughout the world, and to other communities whose heritage is similarly worth conserving.

Such details as cannot be included in a Report designed to have a wide circulation will be made available by the Edinburgh Architectural Association through Amenity Societies, Street Associations, or similarly authoritative bodies.

Reports, however excellent, merely gather dust on library shelves if they do not lead to action.

The Scottish Civic Trust has had the benefit of the advice of W. A. Elliott QC, Mr James Dunbar-Nasmith, Mr Andrew Hughes, Mr Andrew Kerr, Sir Robert Matthew, Mr Ian Ramsay, Mr John Reid, and Sir Thomas Waterlow in appraising the implications of the Edinburgh Architectural Association's Survey. The outcome of the discussions of this group forms the basis of the recommendations which will be put before this Conference, and which are designed to ensure a practical outcome.

HOW THE NEW TOWN OF EDINBURGH CAME INTO BEING

Although, for convenience, the large Georgian unit which is the subject of this Conference is referred to as the New Town, in fact it is made up of a series of New Towns, each one added to the whole over a period of almost a century.

To appreciate the merits of this magnificent piece of extensively planned architectural heritage, it is helpful to know what happened to bring it about.

The growth of the mediaeval town extended eastwards, from the Castle, and funnelled through the narrow Castle Hill into the broader street-scape of the Lawnmarket and the High Street. The mediaeval plan is still readily discernible, but it should be remembered that the original frontages were built to the street and gardens extended to the North Loch, on the North side, and to the Cowgate on the South. The Royal Mile, as we know it, incorporates the separate Royal Burgh of Canongate which operated independently until as recent as 1856.

The character of the Canongate was quite different from that of the area contained within the defensive walls. Open garden ground was in generous proportion to the density of occupation. This resulted in industry moving in to the Canongate and the mediaeval city becoming more and more overcrowded. The area within the defensive region is approximately one quarter mile square. To relieve the chronic over-crowding which had reached the amazing figure of almost seven hundred persons per acre, with an annual mortality rate of thirty-five per thousand, the first extension on any scale was the formation of George Square in 1766, followed quickly by Lord Provost Drummond's scheme for the New Town prepared by James Craig in 1767.

Thereafter events moved fast; the planned expansion, initially for the upper classes, gained ground, to the detriment of the mediaeval city. The vacated houses in the old town were sub-divided into single room units and this in turn gave rise to even more overcrowding. Dr Bell carried out a survey of Blackfriars' Wynd in 1850, and in one hundred and forty-two houses examined, there were one hundred and ninety-three rooms, with one thousand and twenty-five people living in them. This works out at approximately one hundred and ninety cubic feet each, and assuming an average ceiling height of eight feet it is approximately five feet by five feet of floor space per person. These truly shocking conditions culminated in Lord Provost Chambers' reforms and eventually the Improvement Act of 1867, which gave rise to improvements at Market Street, Cranston Street, Jeffrey Street, Blackfriars Street, St Mary's Street and Chambers Street, producing for the first time decent houses for the working class.

Massive improvements of this sort also resulted, of course, in mass destruction of older buildings. To those accustomed to the squalor of the old town, the appearance of Craig's plan must have made a dramatic contrast, and thus the expression 'The New Town' was born. However, there are several New Towns contained within the area of our study and a brief history of each development is now traced. This formed the basis for the eight sub-divisions of the Edinburgh Architectural Association's Survey.

The general plan of the first New Town was laid out by James Craig in 1767. The basic design theme, as in the old town, was the creation of a principal street, following the crown of a ridge, George Street. Strict control was exercised over the feus and all buildings had to conform to a three-storey limitation in height. No building could exceed a wallhead height of forty-eight feet from the basement level, and this concept resulted in neat self-contained residential units. The area comprises Princes Street, George Street, Queen Street, and the terminal squares St Andrew and Charlotte.

The second New Town, the St James' Square area, was started by James Craig in 1775, but this development proceeded without the same stringent control of height, and, indeed, before a comprehensive plan was evolved. Leith Walk, the traditional route from the City to the Port of Leith, has always complicated the plan of the area, and thwarted the original concept of a dignified approach from the East. Broadly this area was completed in 1815 by Robert Stevenson and Archibald Elliot. Thus Waterloo Place and Regent Bridge formed the final approach envisaged in the earlier concept. The area comprises York Place (designed as an extension to Queen Street), Picardy Place, St James' Square, Leith Street, and Waterloo Place. It is convenient here to include the works of Playfair on Calton Hill, Royal, Carlton, and Regent Terraces, and the later development to North Brunswick Street, Windsor Street, and Leopold Place.

The third New Town was designed by Reid and Sibbald in 1802, with Great King Street as the major design unit, terminated at each end by Drummond Place and Royal Circus respectively. Unfortunately, here the natural slope of the ground did not aid the effectiveness of the basic plan. The major difference between the design of this, and Craig's work, with the possible exception of Charlotte Square, is that all the streets are flanked by blocks of unified architectural design. Gap site considerations are clearly much more complicated than in Craig's plan. The area comprises Heriot Row, Abercromby Place, Northumberland Street, Dundas Street, Howe Street, India Street, Gloucester Place, Great King Street,

Royal Circus, Drummond Place, Bellevue Crescent, London Street, Fettes Row, and Royal Crescent.

The fourth New Town was developed, on ground belonging to the Earl of Moray, to the design of James Gillespie Graham in 1822. It has an extremely functional plan which was intended to relate Royal Circus to Charlotte Square, although, again, substantial changes in level physically prevented Gloucester Place from connecting, at road level, to Royal Circus. This plan comprises Doune Terrace, Moray Place, Ainslie Place, Great Stuart Street, and Randolph Crescent.

The fifth New Town (the West End), completed by 1890, was created within the area bounded by Belford Road, Queensferry Street, Shandwick Place (including Atholl Crescent), and Playfair's Donaldson's hospital (1854). Across the Water of Leith, from the Reid and Sibbald development, lies the village of Stockbridge, originally a small village on the river bank, but which has assumed importance because of a series of minor Georgian schemes which developed around it, using it as a focal centre. Thus, though isolated from the major building of the period, particularly important are Ann Street (1823), Danube Street, Carlton Street, Dean Terrace, St Bernard's Crescent (1828), Raeburn Place, St Bernard's Row, Malta Terrace, Saxe Coburg Place, West Claremont Street, Warriston Crescent, Inverleith Row, and Howard Place.

The remaining major development unit to be considered can be called, for the sake of convenience, the sixth New Town. The Learmonth Estate was directly linked with the fourth Town by the completion of Telford's Dean Bridge in 1832. Thus a further major unit was built, bounded by Comely Bank, the Water of Leith, and Orchard Brae. This is an important area because of the large expanse of open spaces connecting Daniel Stewart's College (1853), Fettes College (1870), and the open area extending through to Inverleith.

The orderly growth pattern of the New Town developments culminated suddenly and dramatically with the arrival of the railway network, the most demanding single planning factor in the general upheaval of the Industrial Revolution. Almost overnight, in the second half of the nineteenth century, further expansion on the New Town principle ceased. Several sections were abandoned and sites adapted for industrial use. A notable example is the Silvermills area.

Lord Provost Drummond's original vision is one of the most far-sighted and comprehensive pieces of Georgian planning ever to be executed in this country. It is interesting to note the change in standards, from the comparatively leisurely approach of Craig and his general restrictions in the first New Town, to an increasing acceleration of development; not as residential units for the upper classes, refugees from the old town, but as shaped, social and economic units to suit an ever-expanding City.

Throughout all this development, probably the most notable theme to emerge was that of the Greek Revival Movement, and, at this stage of our assessment, it is perhaps as well to remind ourselves of the words of Henry Russell Hitchcock in *Architecture: Nineteenth and Twentieth Centuries*.

It was in Scotland, not in England, that the Greek revival had its greatest success and lasted longest. There seems to have been such special congruity of sentiment between Northern Europe in the first half of the 19th century and the ancient world. Edinburgh, which considered itself for intellectual reasons 'the Athens of the North', set out after 1810 to continue in a more Athenian mood, the extension and embellishment of her New Town begun in the 1760s. The result rivals Petersburg (i.e. Leningrad) as well as Copenhagen, Berlin and Munich. Indeed, in Edinburgh, what was built between 1760 and 1860 provides still the most extensive example of a romantic classical City in the world.

The architectural form is inter-related throughout all the developments; the subtle siting gives rise to a series of completely unexpected vistas and terminal units; very little of it has reached the advanced state of decay that earlier Georgian Cities, such as Bath, have suffered. There have, of course, been many changes and adjustments to conform with social and economic pressures: for instance, in Princes Street, not one of the original houses has survived unaltered, and indeed, in considering the first New Town, all that remains of any significance are the Public Buildings. Economic erosion has entered into Craig's plan. Thus, the most significant buildings remaining, for instance, in George Street are St Andrew's Church and John Henderson's Assembly Rooms (1784–7).

WHY DOES THE NEW TOWN MATTER?

Covering about a square mile, Georgian Edinburgh is the largest single area of high-quality building in Britain. Its size and its architectural consistency earn it a special place among the planned cities of the world.

The value of the New Town lies in its functional, architectural, and environmental qualities, and it is impossible to separate these three.

The single house (or flatted tenement) is the typical architectural unit of the first New Town in its earlier development. Charlotte Square, at its West End, marks a change. Its North side combines, for the first time in Edinburgh, a row of private houses into the grand civic entity of a palace-fronted terrace. Houses were still built by individual developers, but in conformity with the design and other requirements laid down by the feudal superior. This practice continued to be enforced throughout the construction of the rest of the New Town.

The Charlotte Square theme, a long terrace with prominent ends and centre, was also adopted through most of Georgian Edinburgh.

Sometimes the crowning pediment was omitted from the centre or there was no central emphasis at all—the linking terrace, more or less grandly treated, running continuously between the end blocks. V-jointed masonry was often used for the ground floor, in contrast with the polished or droved stonework of the lofty upper storeys. Major departures from these principles are quite rare and, where they occur, significant.

Many of the end blocks stand on a corner common to two streets. With the repetition of this theme, the built-up island, or composite block, became the characteristic unit of the New Town layout. Some of the corners are handled with particular ingenuity, formed into towers or swept round in a large or small curve.

Within the composite block, the back windows overlook private gardens ('drying greens') and lanes which sometimes give access to mews buildings. While the architecture of the frontages is magnificent, there is no doubt that a great deal of work is needed on the backlands of many New Town properties. In others, there has been piecemeal development (e.g. garages or parking space) which has prejudiced the possibilities of common use and amenity. While this aspect has not been costed, the survey by the architects made it clear that they should on no account be overlooked.

In between the blocks, there are subtly varied views and vistas of spaces beyond, terminating in buildings, monuments, or trees, revealing the open sky, or probably an unexpected section of a large panorama. There is the deployment of monumental layouts on a natural slope; the clear statement of beginning and ending as each development is entered, or viewed from outside. Such are the dominating visual ingredients of the New Town.

The traditional demand for flats, as well as houses, was an important influence in the design of terraces. They are often placed in the prominent sections at the centre and at the ends where big tenement blocks turn the corner and set a fine scale (as in the second New Town) for further tenements stepping boldly downhill.

Housing formed nine-tenths of the total volume of building in the New Town. A decline in the demand for large-scale private houses has been partly off-set by their conversion into hotels and offices and for other semi-public uses. In environmental terms, some of these changed uses are favourable and some are not; indeed they vary from one individual case to another, and are thus all the more difficult to limit, or influence, by planning control. The long-term danger is that non-housing uses may be both transient and irreversible. When an office is no longer needed as such it may be economically difficult to make it into a house again.

The more modest New Town houses have probably never been more fully used than they are today in their proper role; as houses to live in. They are roomy and remarkably flexible in use, without being dauntingly grand. They lack, however, provision for carparking, but the communal conversion of parts of gardens might help to solve what is an inescapably modern problem. A companion study on open spaces is being pursued.

It is a pity that some streets of good houses have been turned over to commercial or industrial use from which they could only be extricated by a major operation of planning and re-conversion. Even in these cases, good architectural quality justifies careful conservation.

In spite of the drawbacks of access by stair, the Georgian flats and maisonettes of the New Town are generally very serviceable, and it is noteworthy that many have been carefully improved and maintained in streets which have a superficially depressed appearance on account of the introduction of mixed uses. Throughout the New Town many basement flats have been ingeniously converted for modern use. They have their own front doors and good lighting on the back elevation.

Both flats and houses have a great wealth of fine detail in their plaster, woodwork, fireplaces, and stair balusters. Well matched to the scale and character of the rooms, they provide a contrast with the relative plainness of the exterior.

On the outside, details and accessories are more sparing but equally important. There is, or should be, very little variation in the overall pattern of astragals in sash windows. The design of fanlights and panelled doors, and such details as railings and balconies (painted black) are much less standardized. All these provide interest and diversity within the unity of a frontage.

Dormer windows, and other more serious excrescences, above the wall-head are sometimes almost as old as the houses themselves. Many dormers are of graceful design, including some with curving, slate-covered cheeks, and have little or no adverse effect on front elevations. Others are clearly obvious intrusions.

Shops in the main streets were not originally provided for in the first New Town, but were soon in demand as this area became the principal commercial centre. Ordinary house frontages were adapted as shops, or more often a single storey extension was built out over the front basement area. Unfortunately, the delicacy of a complete Georgian shop front cannot now be seen in Edinburgh, but there are still many good rows of small shops of the period almost unspoiled. They often boast a continuous cornice and facia supported by regular pilasters, with flats provided overhead.

The re-laying of roads with continuous asphalt, and of footpaths with precast slabs, is undoubtedly a visual loss: but in the New Town area the old natural stone setts on the carriageways have become worn and polished and so present a danger to motor traffic. The old natural flag-stones on the footpaths have also become worn and settled so that they are inconvenient to pedestrians. The cost of replacing these materials has become extremely high and the recent practice has been to use asphalt on the carriageways and artificial stone slabs on the footpaths with colouring to match the old natural stone as nearly as possible. By the use of these modern materials the traditional appearance of the streets has to some extent been lost.

In an attempt to minimize this loss the City Engineer has in recent times relaid some of the footpaths with artificial stone slabs having colours which match fairly successfully the original stone flags. The whinstone setts could be retained in carriageways which will not be carrying much traffic, but the standard is bound to suffer unless special financial arrangements are made to cover the extra high cost of mainte-nance. An example of what can be done exists in Ann Street, but this was only possible because of its narrow width and relatively short length.

NEW LIFE FOR CITY CENTRE

Because people increasingly tend to congregate in urban centres—a tendency expected to reach a point where by the end of the century, eighty per cent of the world's population will be housed in cities, a position we in the United Kingdom are in now—the necessity for com-muting to and from their work is increasing and so is the distance they must travel. But the means for doing so conveniently are not expanding at the same rate. Consequently, in many parts of the world, there has been an awakening of interest in the residential potential of city centres where architectural and environmental qualities make such a state of affairs practically possible.

Edinburgh is fortunate in that its New Town has a high residential use and a still higher potential, provided conservation is carried out thoroughly.

The Alternative. If no action at all were taken to conserve the New Town, its fabric would deteriorate at an increasing rate. After their long span of life, the cost of appropriately repairing the exteriors of buildings which give delight, not only to those who live in them, but to other citizens of Edinburgh and tourists from all over the world, is in the nature of an exceptional capital expense which most owners cannot face unaided. Architectural details would thus not be replaced, and the aesthetic values of the buildings would rapidly decline. It would become increasingly difficult for uncontrolled development to be resisted, and the withdrawal of the residents to more environmentally desirable areas would make it difficult to resist pressures to change the use of their dwellings. Georgian houses converted for commercial or industrial use would then sooner or later be found to be less economic than modern development. The domestic pattern would thus be torn and the damage would inevitably spread.

LIMITATIONS OF THE SURVEY

The Edinburgh Architectural Association Survey has only considered items affecting the architectural appearance and condition of the New Town property, with some comment on landscaping issues. Conservation as a whole involves other major questions, such as general planning policy and traffic strategy, which were outside the scope of the survey, although this is a matter for very deep public concern and involvement.

It is intended that when the Final Conference Report is published, it will provide the detailed basic statistical facts from which an overall policy and conservation scheme, which coordinates the responsibilities of private owners, Local Authority, Government, and the professions concerned, can be evolved. The absence of such an overall plan and policy in the past has, perhaps, been as much of a discouragement to conservation as lack of money.

The current detailed study of the Melville Street area is welcomed and the results could well help to establish standards for the less fortunate parts of our Survey area.

COSTS

Nature of Assessment and Basis of Costs. The aim has been to form a broad overall impression of likely costs, both in total and of the various individual contributing factors.

In a cost consideration of this magnitude, it will be quite obvious that any pretence of accuracy, in regard to individual properties, would be totally misleading. Furthermore, the supporting detailed surveys which would be necessary for accuracy and the publication of the accurate facts would require authority from all the individual property owners within the study area. It was decided at the outset that the objects of the Survey did not require such individual assessment.

The costs reported, therefore, are reasonable guides to the level of expenditure, on average, and the broader the base of the average unit chosen the more reasonable will be the facts. The cost for any single individual property cannot of course be assumed by interpolating from these averages.

A comprehensive detailed examination of each property was not made. The Architects' teams, first, completed a standard proforma in respect of each 'block'. These proformae were then used by the Quantity Surveyor as a basis for the cost.

The Quantity Surveyor then considered property in larger units according to the nature of the architectural composition. This varied from individual buildings to the complete side of a terraced street forming a composite group facade. The Quantity Surveyor made a more detailed inspection of one, perhaps two, properties to which permission for access was obtained. This allowed a fair assessment to be made of the roof and chimney-head condition and to some extent allowed a closer inspection of stonework, although the full extent of stone decay cannot be fully established unless scaffolds are erected. However, the remainder of the unit, being considered by the Quantity Surveyor, was assessed visually from the ground to give an average cost picture.

Overall estimated costs are based on levels pertaining at May 1970. It must be appreciated that each year will add substantially to the cost.

Exclusions. (a) No account has been taken of interior condition including any renovation or repair as a result of external fabric failure. (b) The costs of any improvements to rear areas of properties (i.e. gardens, mews property, etc.) are excluded. (c) No attempt has been made to assess problems of dry rot, or other timber infestations, although any noticeable external defects, or details, which would be likely to escalate these costs were taken into account. (d) Professional fees.

Long Term Improvements. In considering the present state of the property in relation to its original form, it is immediately evident that over the years there has been much undesirable alteration and addition to individual properties; for example, many unsuitable dormer windows and other roof excrescences, inappropriate additions to front entrances, the cement rendering or harling of whole elevations, and so on.

It was considered at the outset that such items should be noted by the Architects to provide not only a record of the present position but to provide a basic record for future policy.

During the Survey, some attempt was made to cost the removal of such items with restoration of the building and while this has been of interest, it is quite evident that, apart from the immense cost involved, the practical possibility of such work ever being carried out, bearing in mind other implications (such as associated internal repairs, reduction in numbers of rooms and, therefore, reduction of value of property) is very unlikely.

The costs therefore exclude such considerations.

Presentation of Costs. While all costs are the summation of individual amounts, a unit is necessary to express a fair average adequately. The unit adopted in the following tables is a 'property' which, for this purpose, is defined as one numbered property in the original plan; this may be a house from basement to roof (e.g. Hill Street) or a main door (basement, ground, and first floors) with separately numbered houses above (e.g. much of North Frederick Street). The unit is not standard because the size of the properties varies widely throughout the study area.

COST DATA

A. Overall Assessment

zone	total cost	no. of properties	property average	relation to general average	
1.	£1,013,273	538	£1,883		−£475
2.	179,771	486	407		−1,951
3.	2,502,583	668	3,746	+£1,388	
4.	182,846	234	781		−1,577
5.	1,461,719	650	2,249		−109
6.	1,890,895	400	4,727	+2,369	
7.	940,079	404	2,327		−31
8.	162,005	161	1,006		−1,352
Total	£8,351,171	3,541	2,358		

B. Analysis of Property Average by Elements for Total Survey

1. Stone Cleaning, Repair and Dressings	£1,592	67·5%
2. Roof Issues	202	8·6
3. Doors and Windows	333	14·1
4. Areas	46	1·9
5. Railings	28	1·2
6. Paint	101	4·3
7. Structural	54	2·3
8. Sundries	4	0·2
	£2,358	100·0

A useful comparison could be made against Gross Annual Values
(i.e. an estimate of rent at which a property might reasonably be expected
to be let on the basis of a landlord repairing Lease) and approximate totals
are shown in table D. It is repeated that the cost for any single property
cannot be assumed by interpolating from these averages.

C. Analysis by Zones and Elements of Property Average by Percentage

zone	stone issues	roof issues	doors and win- dows	areas	railings	paint	struc- tural	sun- dries	total property average
1.	67·9	5·0	18·5	1·9	0·8	4·6	1·1	0·2	£1,883 (100%)
2.	74·0	6·8	5·8	1·4	3·2	5·0	3·9	—	407 (100%)
3.	64·5	11·4	15·5	1·3	0·7	3·9	2·6	0·3	3,746 (100%)
4.	39·9	1·4	47·1	1·7	5·0	4·7	0·2	—	781 (100%)
5.	68·4	6·0	16·3	1·2	1·0	6·5	0·6	—	2,249 (100%)
6.	70·6	9·3	9·7	2·8	1·3	2·1	4·1	—	4,727 (100%)
7.	72·9	8·3	6·1	3·3	1·2	5·9	2·1	0·3	2,327 (100%)
8.	58·5	14·7	17·9	1·6	4·7	2·6	—	—	1,006 (100%)

D. Comparison with Total Gross Annual Value

zone	total cost	approximate total G.A.V.	number of years G.A.V. representing total repair cost
1.	£1,013,273	£763,370	1·32
2.	197,771	132,557	1·49
3.	2,502,583	170,914	14·64
4.	182,846	91,377	2·00
5.	1,461,719	384,687	3·79
6.	1,890,895	83,189	22·73
7.	940,079	100,531	9·35
8.	162,005	20,783	7·79
Total	£8,351,171	£1,747,408	4·77

RECOMMENDATIONS

Legal and Administrative. These recommendations under this heading
indicate a possible organization that might be adopted to deal with the
problem of aiding repairs to and restoration of property in the New
Town, and the methods by which such repairs and restoration might
be done.

It seems desirable that any machinery devised for the purpose of assisting owners in the New Town of Edinburgh should be closely linked to the Corporation and the Historic Buildings Council for Scotland. It seems unlikely that the Government or the Corporation would agree that any new free-standing body should be created under statute for the purpose. It is therefore proposed that an Advisory Committee for the conservation of the New Town of Edinburgh should be established consisting of representatives nominated by the Corporation, Historic Buildings Council for Scotland, the Cockburn Association (Edinburgh Civic Trust), the National Trust for Scotland, the Scottish Civic Trust, and the Scottish Georgian Society, and two independent members. The body should be a small executive organization and need not have more than fourteen members, and should have powers to co-opt. Such an Advisory Committee already exists for the same purposes in the City of Bath and is comprised of four City Councillors, two representatives of the Bath Preservation Trust, two members of the Historic Buildings Council, and two independent members. Having regard to the greater area and number of buildings involved, it is clear that the Edinburgh scheme will be on a completely different scale than the Bath one, and will require appropriate servicing

The functions of this New Town Advisory Committee would be to advise the appropriate authorities on the measures necessary to maintain the New Town: but the Advisory Committee would not supercede the Corporation's planning functions. The Advisory Committee would, however, administer such money as may be raised by public appeal.

The Corporation now has power under the Civic Amenities Act 1967 to make grants towards the repair and maintenance of buildings of historic or architectural interest. In the case of Bath, the Government has agreed with the Local Authority a financial sharing arrangement which in that case means a fifty per cent contribution by the Government and twenty-five per cent by the Local Authority, with twenty-five per cent contribution from the owners. In the situation of Edinburgh, the major financial participation arrangements must be worked out primarily between the Government and the Local Authority.

Given the scale of the finance involved it seems unlikely that a blanket scheme of non-contributory grants applying throughout the whole area would be acceptable to the authorities who would have to provide the necessary funds. In some areas the need is greater and the owners less able to contribute than in others. Some property owners may choose to proceed with the work without recourse to grant. Improvement Grants are available, and there is scope for 'improvement' not only by the Government and others but also for activity by Housing Associations. The Government have given detailed advice about this in their *Bulletin*

No. 2 of the New Scottish Housing Handbook (HMSO, 55p), although the stated standards would seem to be minimal.

A scheme might therefore be developed which ran from total purchase or renewal down to loans.

Grants would normally cover only a proportion of the total expenditure and owners would be expected to make a reasonable contribution. Grants would probably be made upon the understanding that all necessary repairs to the building would be carried out, otherwise there would be the risk that expenditure on one part would be rendered ineffective by decay in other parts of the building, such as the roof. Grants for modernization or improvement can sometimes be obtained from the Corporation under existing arrangements.

The Advisory Committee would need some form of permanent secretary.

It will be important to encourage existing New Town Street Associations and to help form others where they do not presently exist. These Associations could be of assistance to the Advisory Committee in creating the climate in which owners would be encouraged to make improvements to their property and to undertake on a community basis surveys of the property in their streets. The Scottish Georgian Society could also render similar assistance as well as the Cockburn Association. The Committee should be empowered to give assistance from time to time to work being done by the various amenity Associations which makes a direct contribution to the central objective.

Architectural. When the New Town Advisory Committee has been established, its first task should be to establish a set of standards which will form the brief to the professional adviser acting on behalf of specially formed Street Committees. These standards should include the whole setting as well as the buildings themselves and they should extend over areas adjoining the areas of major architectural interest to ensure a proper transition in scale, colour, and height where development is permitted.

The Survey area consists of over 200 streets and it is recommended that each street should form a unit for consideration. It is accepted, however, that flexibility will be needed to cope with particular situations or isolated buildings.

The 'street scheme' study should include: (1) A complete assessment, together with proposals in detail, for the following elements: Facades, Roofs, Doors and Windows, Areas, Railings, Paintwork. (2) A detailed use survey. (3) Car parking proposals. (4) An internal survey noting the structural condition including those features which merit conservation and those which require renovation. (5) A report on communal gardens where applicable and consideration given to appropriate replanting. (6) Proposals for road surfaces, pavements, lighting.

Financial. 1. According to the Architects' estimated cost as at May 1970, for total conservation, allowing for stone repair and replacement by natural stone amounts to approximately £8·5 million.

2. It must be assumed that it would not be practicable to carry through the work in a lesser period than twenty years, taking into account the availability of craftsmen and building materials.

3. In twenty years, if nothing is done now, the present estimate of £8·5 million would certainly be £20 million. It is desirable that work would start in the near future, and it is estimated that an appropriate addition to the figure of £8·5 million to allow for inflation might be £6 million, making the cost to be reckoned with approximately £15 million.

4. For example on a basis that the Historic Buildings Council would pay fifty per cent, the Local Authority twenty-five per cent, and the property owners twenty-five per cent, the £15 million quoted above would be:

H B C	7·5	= 0·375	per annum
Local Authority	3·75	= 0·187	per annum
Owners	3·75	= 0·187	per annum
		0·750	per annum.

It must be appreciated that the foregoing figures are averaged over twenty years and that the cost in earlier years will be less than in the later, because of inflation.

5. It seems desirable to raise a Fund on a United Kingdom basis, the New Town of Edinburgh being the most extensive still intact example of Georgian architecture in Britain. It is anticipated that a possible maximum obtainable through such an Appeal might be £500,000. This sum could be used as a revolving fund for the Advisory Committee to provide loans at special rates of interest. It might also be used as a revolving fund for purchase, restoration, and resale.

6. Nothing will provide a greater stimulus towards Conservation than the existence of some completed street schemes. The enthusiasm of property owners and Street Associations will inevitably determine which streets are tackled first, and their example will soon be followed by others when the results are seen.

A GUIDELINE TO THE GEORGIAN PERIOD

1714 Accession of George I.
      Population of Edinburgh, 25,000.
1724 Lord Provost Drummond proposes 'extensions to the north'.
1725 James Court, James Brownhill.
1728 Robert Adam born.
      Music Society of Edinburgh formed.
1738 Infirmary (now demolished), William Adam.
1739 Scots Magazine founded.
1740 James Craig born.
1746 Defeat of second Jacobite rising.
1752 Proposals for carrying on certain Public Works in the City.
1753 Act of Parliament for improving streets and access, and new
      public buildings.
      Royal Exchange (now City Chambers), J. Adam.
1759 Draining North Loch started.
1763 Northern access planned.
      North Bridge (now replaced), W. Mylne.
      Layout of George Square, James Brown.
1766 Competition for 'Plans of a New Town' won by James Craig.
1767 Act for Extension of City.
      Population of Edinburgh, 50,000.
      First New Town.
1772 Act for Lighting and Cleansing.
1774 Register House started, Robert Adam.
1775 St James Square, James Craig.
1777 James Gillespie Graham born.
      Robert Reid born.
1783 Work started on Mound.
1784 Assembly Rooms, J. Henderson.
      Thomas Hamilton born.
1785 Act for South Bridge and College (University) of Edinburgh.
1789 University of Edinburgh, R. Adam.
      William Henry Playfair born.
1790 Forth and Clyde Canal completed.
1791 Charlotte Square, R. Adam.
      Gayfield Place, James Begg.
1799 York Place.
1800 Picardy Scheme, R. Burn.
1801 Population of Edinburgh, 67,000.
1802 Second New Town, R. Reid and W. Sibbald (City Architect).

1812   Competition for layout of Calton Hill.
1813   West End layout, James Gillespie Graham (elevations by various architects).
1815   Eastern access planned, Calton Bridge scheme, A. Elliot.
        West Extension planned.
1816   Act against building on south side of Princes Street.
1818   Gas Lamps introduced.
1819   Calton Scheme, W. Playfair.
        Rutland Square, A. Elliot (not built until 1830/40, John Tait).
1822   Royal Institution (now RSA), W. Playfair.
        Union Canal completed.
        Moray Estate scheme, J. Gillespie Graham.
1823   Royal Circus, William Henry Playfair.
1824   St Bernard's Crescent, James Milne.
1825   Blacket Place, James Gillespie Graham.
1826   Royal High School, T. Hamilton.
        Act approved St Leonards, Dalkeith railway.
1829   Dean Bridge, T. Telford.
1830   Death of George IV
        Population of Edinburgh, 136,000.

ACKNOWLEDGEMENTS

The Scottish Civic Trust wishes to acknowledge the close collaboration it has received from the Civic Trust, London, in the organization and financing of this Conference.

The generosity of the members of the Edinburgh Architectural Association and those who worked with them in the compilation of the Report cannot be warmly enough praised.

The Trust acknowledges, with thanks, the kindness of the Lord Provost of Edinburgh in providing a Reception for those attending the Conference, and expresses its gratitude to the Corporation for the donation covering the hire of the Assembly Rooms. At the same time we thank the Corporation for their assistance with the Survey and in particular the loan of accommodation for the photographs.

The Trust has greatly appreciated the moral and practical support of the University of Edinburgh and in particular the kindness of the Principal in providing a reception for members of the Edinburgh Architectural Association taking part in the Survey.

The Scottish Civic Trust was particularly pleased to have had the help of the Graphics Department of Edinburgh College of Art, in the preparation of its symbol and typographical material, and wishes to thank the

Head of the Department, Mr Andrew Chisholm, as well as Mr Douglas Baty, who devised the design work.

The Trust thanks the National Trust for Scotland and the Historic Buildings Council for Scotland for their financial assistance towards the cost of the Survey.

The Trust thanks the Managing Director of Messrs Eadie Cairns, Mr John Milne, for the generous gift of wine which accompanied the Conference lunch.

Mrs Kathleen Macfie, the Street Associations, and those who assisted as hostesses are gratefully thanked for the experience of living in the New Town which they offered to Conference guests.

The Managing Director of Messrs George Outram, Mr Alan Stephen, is thanked for his kindness in making available re-prints of the *Scottish Field* article, 'The Saving of Georgian Edinburgh'.

The Scottish Civic Trust has been grateful for the support of the National Trust for Scotland, the Cockburn Association (Edinburgh Civic Trust), the Scottish Georgian Society, and the Saltire Society throughout this operation.

The Corporation Parks Department have our thanks for kindly providing the flowers and for their help in the open spaces appraisal.

A conference of this size could not be successfully run without the assistance of stewards. The Trust thanks those members of the Edinburgh Architectural Association, and others, who have performed this function.

We are grateful to Messrs Law & Dunbar-Nasmith who mounted the special Exhibition on show in the Assembly Rooms.

The following are the members of the New Town Survey Team of the Edinburgh Architectural Association, responsible for carrying out a survey of the external fabric of some five thousand properties in the New Town.

Town Planning Amenity Committee. John H. Reid (Convener), George A. Macnab, Andrew Kerr, T. Harley Haddow, John V. Ramsay (Technical Secretary), David P. Ross, Peter Graham, Colin McWilliam, Peter W. Dixon, Christine McWilliam (Organizing Secretary).
In addition the Chairmen of the eight zones served in the main Committee.

Group 1. Charles T. Donaldson (Chairman), Donald McInnes, John Thyne, Richard Jaques, Ronald Malcolm, W. C. Fraser, Mr and Mrs A. Findlay, M. J. Slater, Anthony Pearson, John V. Gardner, M. Duncan, Douglas Hogg, Robert Ogilvie, Andrew Yool, Angus Robertson, G. N. Gardiner.

Group 2. David E. Witham, J. Fullarton (Joint Chairmen); D. Stein, M. R. Miller, W. Sinclair, Ian D. McNeill, Alex J. Brown, Roy G. Jardine, W. McMaster, A. S. Taylor, P. J. Robinson, I. K. N. Smith, N. Ewan, T. Pollock, Mrs J. L. Busby, Peter Oliver, D. D. Sutherland, D. D. Quinn, J. C. Shorney, R. A. Knox.

Group 3. Stanley P. Ross-Smith (Chairman), J. H. Clark, Anthony Forward, Michael W. Jeffrey, Judith Pickles, Isa Ross, John Sutherland, James D. Wren, T. G. Pottie.

Group 4. Leslie Jones (Chairman), Dorothy Miller, Eric Hall, A. McLean, D. Taylor, N. L. Glen, C. Girdler, Arthur Lowes, M. F. Conn, R. A. Robertson, A. D. Hardie.

Group 5. Ian Gordon (Chairman), James Taylor, George Gourlay, V. Campden, J. Orgel, Ian Begg, Alastair M. Smith, Peter Allam, T. H. Duncan, R. Nimmo, Gordon Moses, D. Lauder, K. Tarbet, G. F. Robertson, J. Hunt, J. R. Dawson

Group 6. J. C. Mackay (Chairman), Eric Dawson, J. Mitchell, D. McGill, M. Lee, A. Sneddon, Keith P. Durrant, David Price, E. W. Marchant, David Gillespie, David Gemmell, Neil Hynd, George Bethune, J. L. Bremner.

Group 7. J. E. C. Campbell (Chairman), Miss M. White, Charles B. Swan, Ian Douglas, Fiona Mason, W. P. Dickson, Scott Bennett, Alec Laughlan, Jim Meikle, D. J. H. Muir, J. P. Fyfe.

Group 8. J. R. Oberlander (Chairman), J. D. Spencely, Mary Tindall, M. S. Higgs, T. A. Jamieson, Tony Winkle, R. T. Morrison.

Photographic Team. David Hamilton, Richard Andrews, Alastair L. Hunter, Rosemary Hunter, Ron Morrison, George L. Stevens, Morva Smith, Matthew Turnbull.